POLICY-MAKING IN THE GERMAN FEDERAL BUREAUCRACY

Policy-Making in the German Federal Bureaucracy

Renate Mayntz

University of Cologne, Cologne, Germany

Fritz W. Scharpf

International Institute of Management, Berlin, Germany

Elsevier

Amsterdam - Oxford - New York 1975

ELSEVIER SCIENTIFIC PUBLISHING COMPANY
335 Jan van Galenstraat
P.O. Box 211, Amsterdam, The Netherlands

and

52 Vanderbilt Avenue,
New York, New York 10017

Cc.

Library of Congress Card Number: 74-21862

ISBN 0-444-41272-7

Printed in The Netherlands

CONTENTS

FOREWORD

This book is basically an empirical monograph about policy-making processes and their structural determinants in one specific setting. Though we have taken into account that many of its readers will not be familiar with this setting and have tried to supply the essential descriptive information, the aim of the book is not to present a comprehensive survey of the German Federal Republic's system of government. Again, though we have set our analysis in a theoretical frame of reference, which is developed in the first two chapters, our aim has not been an extensive theoretical discussion. This is also evident from the lack of extended references to the relevant literature which the reader will soon notice.

Speaking generally, ours is a structural-functional, or systems approach. As is known, this approach permits to stipulate normative reference points for an empirical analysis, whether these are derived from the values of system members or some value standard of the analyst. Our normative point of reference is the conviction, shared today by scientists of widely differing political affiliations, that in highly developed modern societies the active direction of social and economic processes by the political sub-system has become a basic condition of system survival. Hence we ask for the prerequisites of a high directive capacity. Active political direction meets with restrictions external to the political system, which we discuss briefly. Our main interest, however, is in the question how, given these external restrictions, the structure and mode of operation of the policy-making system influences the quality of policy output. For reasons elaborated in detail in chapter III, this question directs attention specifically to the structure and functioning of the federal bureaucracy, which thus becomes the focal object of our analysis.

Though this book may lack the outward appearance of an empirical monograph, i.e. percentage figures in the text, tables, correlation coefficients, and interview excerpts, it is in fact based upon the results of several empirical investigations which the authors undertook either jointly or separately. These studies include: an organizational analysis of the Federal Press and Information Office; several case studies of policy decision processes at the federal level; two case studies of the influence of external groups on executive planning; a study of patterns of inter- and intra-departmental coordination; a large-scale investigation of civil service careers and attitudes; and most importantly, an extensive empirical study of policy-making structures and processes in five federal ministries. All of these studies were done under government research contracts, most of them being closely connected with specific reform endeavours. The research reports have generally been made available to restricted audiences in mimeographed form, but were not published except for the civil service study. In this book we do not reproduce these research reports — which, incidentally, would not even be a very meaningful enterprise — but we draw on the cumulative store of information jointly produced by these several studies. In addition, we have of course made use of research results reported by other investigators. But wherever no other source is explicitly given for a certain observation or factual statement, it derives from one of the studies previously mentioned or from knowledge which the authors gained in the course of their political counseling activities, their membership and work in various governmental reform commissions, and through contacts thus established.

In our empirical studies we were assisted by a number of young researchers, all of whom we want to thank sincerely. Out of their number we mention especially those four persons who have worked with us longest and who have contributed most to the production of the ideas and empirical data utilized for this book: Hanfried Andersen, Hans-Ulrich Derlien, Jurgen Küssau, and Hubert Treiber. We also wish to thank summarily our many respondents and discussion partners from the federal executive, and our secretaries who typed the several versions of this book.

Köln and Berlin, May 1974

Renate Mayntz, Fritz W. Scharpf

Chapter I

INTRODUCTION

The substance of this book will deal with policy-making procedures, organization, and personnel in the German federal bureaucracy. But our interest in these structural patterns is defined within the wider frame of reference of the ability of political systems to deal effectively with the range, the order of magnitude and the dynamic instability of the problems generated in highly developed, "post industrial" Western societies. As will become clear later on, we regard present bureaucratic policy-making structures as one major constraint upon the problem solving capacity of the West German political system, on which we have focussed our study. But they are not the only operative constraints, and they operate within a wider context of facilitating and restrictive conditions which determine their relative significance. Thus we begin a cursory examination of the wider context within which the bureaucracy must operate.

1. Problem-solving as a problem

The capacity of political systems in post industrial, Western societies to cope with an increasing problem load has become doubtful. There is a widespread impression, shared by politicians, administrators, social scientists and, increasingly, the informed public, that we seem to be falling behind, rather than catching up with our most urgent problems. And the gap seems to widen, the faster we run. The more highways are built, the more they are congested; the more we invest in urban renewal, the more our cities seem to turn into commercial wastelands; the more money we spend on higher education, the more urgent are the reports of crises at our universities; the more people we employ in the public

1

sector, the more we are dissatisfied with the quality of our public services. This increasing sense of crisis is merely dramatized by the warnings of an impending ecological disaster, which tell us that unless we should be able to stop quantitative economic growth, resource consumption and environmental pollution within the next few decades, human civilization as we have known it can no longer be supported on this planet [1].

We have come to realize that we are paying the price of growth in terms of traffic congestion, urban decay, and environmental pollution, or in terms of the social nonintegration of millions of foreign workers and their families, or of the relative poverty and misery in backward regions, or in industries and skill groups left behind by technological and economic progress. And we also begin to see high rates of alienation, mental disorder, drug addiction, suicide, crime and rebellion as part of the social costs of rapid change and dislocation. And while we are still struggling to understand the problems generated by the rapid economic growth of the last decades, the energy crisis has forced upon us the awareness that non-growth by itself will not be a solution but will confront us with even less manageable problems of stagflation, structural unemployment, economic strife, and political unrest caused by the sudden disappointment of long-internalized expectations of continuing material betterment.

The list could easily be extended. But we need not go on. The problem load generated by modern economies and societies seems staggering. And while societal problems and dysfunctions may be absorbed at the level of the individual, the family, or the private enterprise system, such sub-political problem-solving mechanisms seem to have lost much of their effectiveness or tend to displace rather than solve the underlying problems. As a consequence, societal problems have become 'politicized' at least in the sense that their solution is increasingly dependent upon the compensatory action or intervention of political systems that have, everywhere, assumed ever-increasing responsibilities for the management of socio-economic processes.

At the same time, modern societies, through the concurrent evolution of education, mass communication, science and social criticism have become much more sensitive to their problems and have continuously increased the level of expectations by which they evaluate the actual performance of social systems. And they also have, through general elections, political strikes and demonstrations, the mass-media, pressure groups, and competitive party systems, developed powerful mechanisms for translating levels of manifest demand and perceived societal problems into issues on the agenda of political systems. For all practical purposes, modern Western societies and policies have effectively lost the option of 'benign neglect'. They cannot ignore societal problems even though they may be quite incapable of effective solution. The seeming discrepancy between the problem-generating tendencies of modern societies and the problem-solving capacities of their political systems thus emerges as a question of immense practical as well as theoretical interest.

2. Critical demands upon the political system

Perhaps the problem of inadequate problem-solving capacity needs to be formulated at a high level of generality if we assume that specific deficiencies in system performance have a tendency to spread beyond narrow sectors and to turn into generalized system crises. Still, it is not easy to see how solutions might be usefully discussed at such a level of generality. Problems tend to arise in certain fields and sectors: urban development, education, unemployment, balance of payments, or inflation. And problems tend to be handled by similarly specialized policy sub-sets of the political system. In any modern political system, the actual (or, at any rate, the perceived) overlap between problems and problem-solving systems in different areas, say, preschool education and the development of new sources of energy, tends to be minimal. It is therefore not obvious that statements about deficiencies of pro-blem-solving capacity could be generalized across many fields, and that anything but a detailed discussion of problem-generating ten-dencies and problem-solving mechanisms for each narrow field by itself would add much to our understanding.

While we regard such substantive problem and policy analyses as necessary, we also know how difficult it is to do them well on narrow problem areas, and how rapidly the difficulties approach impossibility when the focus is extended toward a macro-societal perspective — provided that one will not fall back to a dogmatic Marxist or Neo-Marxist position which defines the capitalist or-ganization of the economy as the source of all societal problems and its abolition as the universal solution. Thus, as long as we wish to deal with the political system of the Federal Republic of Ger-many as a whole, or even with the federal government as its subsystem, it is clearly impossible to base any deficiency analysis upon a substantive analysis of the specific economic and societal problems that would require political solution. Instead, we have chosen a more abstract approach. We assume without further discussion or justification that the most urgent problems confronting governments under modern conditions will have some extremely abstract characteristics in common, and that solutions to these problems will require policies which can, again, be characterized by some highly abstract qualities upon which their effectiveness will depend. They, in turn, may be translated into a set of more specific structural prerequisites which a policy-making system must possess in order to generate the kind of policies which may have a chance of coping effectively with the problem-generating tendencies of modern societies. After these structural requisites have been established, it is then possible to talk more concretely and specifically about policy-making structures in the West German political system and about structural deficiencies that might impair their problem-solving capacity.

We take as our starting point a few basic assumptions about the problem-generating characteristics of postindustrial societies. They include a high degree of differentiation among specialized structures and processes in the socio-economic system with a correspondingly high degree of functional interdependence among these specialized sectors; they also include high rates of technological, economic, cultural and social change, as well as the expectation that such processes of change may rapidly approach critical boundaries defined by the exhaustion of scarce resources, the disruption of ecological or social balances, and the limitations of human tolerance for insecurity and frustration. The approach toward these critical boundaries may often result from the cumulative effects of seemingly unrelated and individually innocuous processes.

Policies that might deal effectively with highly differentiated, highly interrelated and rapidly changing, 'turbulent' environment [2], can, again, be characterized in a highly abstract fashion:

(1) The differentiation and connectedness of the underlying societal sub-processes require a corresponding degree of complexity at the policy level [3]. Policies need to be specific with regard to the specific conditions of differentiated sectors — they tend to be ineffective to the extent that they must aggregate their response across all or many sectors. At the same time, however, effective policy-making must also respond to

the connectedness of differentiated sectors. As manifest problems in one area may be caused by conditions, and may themselves affect conditions, in other sectors, isolated policies aimed directly at manifest symptoms may be quite ineffective or may even increase rather than reduce the total problem load of the system.

(2) The dynamic character of problem-generating processes and the requisite complexity of solutions combine to increase the minimal timespan required for effective policies. Dynamic processes — like population growth or industrial dislocations — can rarely be stopped or changed abruptly; and in complex solutions the interrelated elements will have specific lead times of their own which may combine into a critical path that will not permit for any short-term solutions to urgent, manifest problems. Thus, effective policy-making will have to be future-oriented and will increasingly depend upon medium- and long-range forecasting and policy-planning capabilities.

(3) If dynamic social-economic processes should approach toward critical boundaries of ecological, social, or individual systems capacity, effective solutions need to change the speed and the direction of such processes. Even complex and future-oriented policies which are merely adaptive or facilitative in relation to the underlying societal processes — as most public infra-structure policies in the past have tended to be — may in effect help to accelerate and exacerbate, rather than to reduce or avoid crisis conditions. Effective solutions increasingly depend upon the capacity to direct and control socioeconomic processes.

(4) Political problem-solving processes will not achieve substantive control of societal processes unless they can maintain a high degree of relative autonomy from any specific societal interests. As the perspective of each economic or social group or subsystem will tend to be much narrower than the existing network of interrelated problem sectors, any policy which would tie itself to the interests and perspectives of any single group or sector would tend to be sub-optimal and might be self-defeating. If this is true, there may be objective reasons for preferring political structures which are less, rather than more, responsive to the articulated demands of societal groups and sub-systems. Such a requirement lies uneasily with the normative and empirical need for democratic legitimacy, and it raises difficult theoretical and practical questions which cannot be pursued here. [4]

5

The demands for more complex, long-range, controlling, and autonomous policies — in short: for more *active* rather than *reactive* policy-making — need to be translated into structural prerequisites before existing political systems can be evaluated in these terms. That will be the task of the next chapter. At this point, however, we should remind ourselves of the abstractness of our basic assumptions. We have assumed that there are important problem-generating processes in society which call for complex, long-range, controlling, and autonomous policies if severe crises are to be avoided. But we cannot say that *all* societal processes are of this kind. There are still relatively isolated sub-systmes of society in stable equilibrium or slow change where, if problems should arise, limited, short-range, adaptive, and responsive policy-making may be fully sufficient, and where any hyper-activity of the political system might do more harm than good. Thus, political systems need to maintain their capacity for reactive policy-making. And even where active policy-making is required, the demands upon the capacities of the system will vary considerably from one area to the next and even from one problem to the next within the same area. Thus, the following elaboration of the structural prerequisites of active policy-making should be read as a list of maximum, rather than average requirements.

We focus upon them because they seem critical in two respects: we expect that unless these prerequisites are fulfilled, the most dynamic and potentially most destructive societal process cannot be effectively contained; and we also expect that the prerequisites of active policy-making are much more difficult to provide within the political system than are the conditions of reactive policies. But we certainly do not assume that all, or even most, policy-making need or should be active policy-making, even under the conditions of post-industrial societies. [5]

In the following chapter we will elaborate the prerequisites of active policy-making. While these categories are still developed in an abstract and theoretical fashion, we also intend to use the chapter in order to sketch in the context for the subsequent analysis of policy-making structures in the Federal Republic of Germany. For that reason, we will increasingly illustrate general propositions through specific examples without, however, attempting any systematic or exhaustive description of the West German societal and political system. [6]

Chapter II

THE PREREQUISITES
OF ACTIVE POLICY-MAKING

Under present conditions, active policy-making in the Federal Republic will be primarily federal policy-making or, at least, policy-making with federal involvement. State and local governments are too restricted in their legislative authority and in their financial resources to be able to develop problem-solving capacities commensurate with the scope of the most pressing problems. However, as will be made clear in later sections, they will be typically involved in the formulation and in the execution of federal policies.

Within the federal political system, our primary focus will be upon the 'active policy-making system' or action system comprising that subset of actors whose contributions will effectively determine the substance of national policies. It includes the party organizations of the government coalition, their parliamentary parties, parliament and its committees, the *Bundesrat*, and the federal government comprising the cabinet and the federal bureaucracy. While policy proposals may originate elsewhere, they must be accepted, processed and converted into government policy within the action system. Thus, for most purposes of analysis, it seems useful to us to focus upon this sub-system, and to treat all other factors affecting policy-making as part of its environment.

The problem-solving capacity of the action system is dependent upon resources which may be classified in a variety of ways. For our purposes, we have found a classification into the four categories of financial, informational, organizational and political resources most useful. Still, any classification which attempts completeness must draw some arbitrary lines. In our case, for instance, we do include the scope of government authority among the organizational resources, and the skills and motivations of available personnel which surely are among the most important policy resources, will be dealt with in chapter IV describing the federal bureaucrats. We have chosen the present emphasis because we regard financial resources, information and decision-making technology, the organizational capacity for action in a differentiated political structure, and the political capacity to build support and to regulate conflict as, at the same time, very scarce resources of the political system and very important preconditions of active policy-making.

To some extent these resources must be supplied as inputs from the external socio-economic environment into the political system; to some extent they can be produced within the political system itself; and in most cases the ability of the political system to effectively utilize available resources must itself be regarded as an important internal resource. But as the internal structural prerequisites will concern us throughout the major part of this study, we will here concentrate primarily upon the environmental conditions which determine the availability of external resources.

1. Financial prerequisites

Active policy-making is generally characterized by rising demands upon financial resources. This seems to reflect a general trend in Western societies which, however, may be reinforced by the prevailing modalities of political problem-solving. If direct, imperative control of private decisions and behavior is restricted by constitutional and socio-cultural norms and, in many areas, would be prohibitively expensive in terms of political support; and if the information base and the methodology for the indirect control of socio-economic processes are insufficiently developed, active policy-making is primarily left with only one problem-solving modality: the direct supply of goods, services and investments by the government itself. Obviously, from the point of view of government finances, this is also the most expensive problem-solving modality. [1]

In the Federal Republic, economic growth rates had been exceptionally high in the nineteen-fifties and early nineteen-sixties. In addition, the conservative fiscal policy of the fifties had accumulated large financial reserves which, in the late fifties and early sixties resulted in rapidly expanding spending programs. [2] As a consequence, the first serious economic recession of 1966/67

8

also caused a severe fiscal crisis on all levels of government, federal, state and local. While the recession was overcome fairly rapidly with the help of massive programs of deficit-spending, growth rates have fluctuated since then and the demands upon public finances have increased rapidly in a number of policy areas which had been badly neglected during the reconstruction period and the early sixties. In education, for instance, expenditures have risen from DM 16.8 Billion in 1965 to DM 38.7 Billion in 1972 and are projected to reach DM 100 Billion in 1980. Similar projections have been made in the areas of transportation, of urban renewal and housing, of the health services or of pollution control. [3] As a consequence and in spite of widespread misgivings about the effects upon the ecological balance and the quality of life, the stimulation of economic growth at the rate of 5% p.a. remains a policy priority to which the reform-oriented Social Democratic Party firmly committed itself in the draft of its long-range program for 1973 to 1985. In addition, the party projects a rise in the governmental share of GNP from a rate of 27.9% in 1970 to 33.9% in 1985. [4]

Finally, the use of available resources is restricted by the dual function of public spending as an instrument of financing substantive public policy and as an instrument of anti-cyclical economic policy. The Federal Republic was rather late in recognizing this second, neo-Keynesian function of the budget in its 'Economic Stabilization Act' adopted in the aftermath of the recession of 1966/67. But while its expansionary instruments could be used with impressive success during the first two years after the recession, a booming economy and growing rates of inflation after 1968 have severely restrained the expansion of public budgets. At the same time, the continuous inflow of foreign capital caused by expectations of further revaluations of the D-mark reduced the effectiveness of the classical instruments of monetary policy, high interest rates and credit limitations. Thus, the major burden of inflation control fell upon the new instruments of fiscal policy, and the burden had to be borne primarily by the federal budget. The "Economic Stabilization Act" of 1967 had provided only for the voluntary coordination of federal, state, and local fiscal policy, and therefore state and local governments in effect continued to be much more concerned with the balance of their revenues and expenditures, contracting their budgets when revenues were low and expanding them with the rising tax levels of an accelerating economy.

9

The problem became acute only after the elections of 1969 which the Social Democrats had fought on the inflation issue and which squarely confronted them with political responsibility for inflation control which, under the circumstances, had to be achieved primarily through constraints upon the federal budget. Such constraints were felt all the more severly by a government coalition which had entered office with an extremely ambitious and costly program of 'domestic reforms'. During the following years, the government was unable to resolve this conflict between its economic and political goals in one way or another, ending up with unprecedented rates of inflation and with the disappointment of reformist hopes at the same time. The high inflation rates of all western economies during the same period suggest that much of this development may have been beyond governmental control. Nevertheless, the extent to which the costs of inflation were borne by reformist policies also suggests that some of the blame should rest with a system of fiscal management which makes it particularly difficult to reallocate available resources according to shifting political priorities. These and other problems of existing patterns of internal resource utilization will be discussed below in chapter VIII, 1. [5]

2. Informational prerequisites

Different modalities of governmental problem-solving vary in their informational requirements. The requirements are obviously minimized in a pattern of merely reactive policy-making which relies on explicit and politically articulated demands from the socio-economic environment to signal manifest problems and crises. This type of ad hoc problem-solving requires relatively little predictive knowledge. The opposite is true of active policy-making, for which by and large the same informational requirements can be said to hold which have been discussed as prerequisites of long-term, large-scale, comprehensive planning. There is no need to repeat here in detail what is familiar from planning theory. [6] Summarized briefly, active policy-making requires knowledge of system dynamics, [7] knowledge which permits contingent predictions of future developments. Predictions of "spontaneous" developments as well as predictions of the consequences of deliberate intervention depend on two types of knowledge: causal knowledge about the connections and interdependencies between separate processes and system parts, and descriptive knowledge (or data) about the present state of the system or relevant system parts. While these requirements hold for active policy-making in general, the informational requirements seem to differ depending on the predominant mode of governmental control. At first sight it may appear that the control of societal processes through the direct, imperative regulation of individual behavior, while associated with high demands upon consensus and enforcement capacities, requires only relatively little empirical information. Where the government can command what people shall do, it might be argued, there is little need to know what people tend to do in given situations. This may well hold for isolated instances of imperative control. But where a large social system is to be controlled in this way in every detail, where a society is to be directed deterministically as it were, a correspondingly detailed and complete knowledge of system interdependencies is required. To overstate the case a bit crudely: where a political leadership attempts to control a society as an engineer constructs and runs a machine, i.e. by designing it to achieve certain goals and assigning all parts their proper place and function, full knowledge is needed of the preconditions as well as of the consequences, manifest and latent, of the intended operation of all system parts, or else the machine will not run, i.e. the aggregate effect of individual compliance will not be the outcome desired. [8] For this reason the informational requirements of a system of imperative control are in fact extremely high, so high as to seriously overstrain existing information-gathering and information-processing capacities. Economic planning in socialist countries might well illustrate this.

Though still formidable enough, the informational requirements of governmental control which operates on the cybernetic principle of manipulating only a few selected control variables are less exacting. This mode of indirect control makes use of incentives and disincentives rather than attempting to determine behavior by direct orders. The avoidance of direct behavior control permits the system to utilize the information-gathering and information-processing capacities of its members, who may react autonomously to "objective" environmental conditions and to existing interdependencies among societal sub-systems. The government can then limit itself to collect that information which permits the identification and manipulation of parameters which affect the general direction of change in the societal sub-systems. The analytical understanding of system dynamics which this requires is still difficult to obtain, but knowledge need at least not be as detailed and complete as in the case of imperative control.

While the substitution of indirect and strategic control for direct and complete control may lower the informational requirements of active policy-making to a level which might conceivably be achieved, we are in many fields still rather far from actually meeting these requirements, both in terms of substantive knowledge and in the technology of information processing. The lack of substantive knowledge is particularly serious in the social sciences. Advances in information technology have so far significantly improved our ability to store massive amounts of data and to perform statistical operations on them. But to gain an understanding of complex system dynamics, techniques of causal modelling and system simulation will have to be devised which are superior to those available now. The work of Forrester has demonstrated the difficulty of the task, but has not yet provided us with techniques that could be effectively used in policy-making. [9]

To emphasize the dependence of active policy-making on data and causal knowledge does not mean to imply that the political system is ignorant without an input of specially prepared information. A substantial amount of (pre-scientific) background information, of "latent", i.e. inexplicit theory, and of empirical knowledge is present in the political system, without making special efforts to collect data and scientific knowledge. It derives in large part from on-going work, from the operation of existing programs and from continuous work on their improvement. Even where the social environment has not yet been sufficiently explored by scientific research, it is therefore not *terra incognita* for the political system. However, the type of information generated by the operation and adaptation of existing programs will rarely be sufficient for active policy-making. Especially where fundamental changes in policy and far-reaching innovations are needed, policy-making remains dependent upon the 'articifical' information produced by scientific research.

In the Federal Republic, scientific research and development which might provide the informational prerequisites of active policy-making have maintained a considerable degree of autonomy — in spite of the fact that universities are state institutions, that much research is directly or indirectly supported by the federal and state governments, [10] and that some specialized disciplines such as agriculture, transportation, or regional science virtually exist only through government sponsorship. With the exception of

12

a few high priority areas like nuclear physics, space research, computer sciences, or marine biology, ongoing research activities can hardly be attributed to any explicit, coherent, and comprehensive research policy of the government. [11] The major purpose of governmental research policy is not to provide an information basis for policy-making, but to support research which seems important, often for economic and ultimately for political reasons such as successful competition in international technological developments, and which is either too costly or not profitable enough to be undertaken and financed by industry. In most other fields, the direction which ongoing research takes is primarily the result of substantive and methodological orientations prevailing within the scientific community itself.

This tendency is supported by the prevailing pattern of scientific organization. Public resources for research are largely distributed through research financing agencies. Most important among these are the *Deutsche Forschungsgemeinschaft* and the *Max-Planck-Gesellschaft*, both of which are legally private institutions though they draw most of their funds from public sources. The typical form of direction of these and other large science organizations in the Federal Republic is cooperative, i.e. representatives of government, science, and industry will sit together in the directing bodies. This excludes full political control, and the avenues for political influence which it provides are often not used in any systematic way.

The stated lack of substantive political control holds particularly for social science research, upon which active policy-making would have to depend heavily. Here the supply of policy-oriented, large-scale, and inter-disciplinary research is generally low and in some important areas practically non-existent. The social sciences exist primarily at overcrowded universities where teaching needs take priority over research in personnel recruitment and in the allocation of time and resources. With the exception of law and economics, most social science departments are quite small and most research is limited to the scale of one or two-man projects, often favoring library research over empirical work. While research budgets in general have increased considerably over the last years in the Federal Republic, the social sciences still receive only a small share of these funds. [12] Connected with this lack of substantial financial support, the choice of research problems is largely determined within the science culture and often does not coincide with the informational needs of public policy-making. In fields like economics, where research capacity seems sufficient and where much of the actual research is related to problems of public policy, the usefulness of existing research for policy-making is restricted by its mono-disciplinary nature which is ill adapted to the multi-dimensional characteristics of real societal problems.

Pointing out the existing limits in the supply of scientific knowledge for policy-making does of course not imply that if only the noted shortcomings could be redressed, the informational needs of policy-making would be fulfilled. For one thing, the availability of needed information does not necessarily mean that it will be utilized. The actual utilization of available information in policy-making processes depends on structural and operational properties of the political system. These include not only factors affecting the internal information-processing capacity, but also the specific modalities of cooperation between the science system and the policy-making system. We shall turn to these questions in chapter VIII. But there is another limit to the fulfillment of informational needs for active policy-making by scientific resarch, which is less a practical question than a matter of principle. There exist inherent limits to the use of scientific information in political decision-making, because more often than not concrete models for action cannot be deduced from scientific analyses, especially where such action involves institution building and affects the societal macro-structure.

In such cases, it is often impossible to anticipate actual effects or the mode of operation of a proposed change or reform, so that experimental research or a form of action research would be necessary. This, however, meets often with resistance from those affected by such experimentation. It may also find little support among politicians who want to realize a particular policy goal which they value for normative and maybe also for strategic reasons, so that they are less interested to inquire beforehand into likely consequences which might dissuade them from their efforts. The recent attempt to resolve the controversy over the general introduction of comprehensive schools in the Federal Republic by instituting a large-scale experimental program in which comprehensive schools are established for test purposes and subjected to scientific observation provides an instructive example for the limitations here briefly alluded to. [13]

3. Organizational prerequisites

The term organization is used here to describe the allocation of authority and policy-making powers to the political system as a whole and their distribution within the political system. For active policy-making, both dimensions are equally important: the first defines the scope of aggregate political authority vis-à-vis the socio-economic environment; while the greater or lesser concentration of powers along the second dimension will determine the relative ease or difficulty with which the aggregate power potential of the political system may be utilized in active policy-making.

3.1 Limits to political authority

In the West German political system like in other Western constitutional democracies, aggregate political power is limited by legal and cultural restraints protecting autonomous societal processes. Among these are, of course, the classical freedoms of religion, of speech and of the press, of suffrage and of assembly, of scientific research and teaching, of movement, of the choice of one's profession, and of property rights. The list of specific constitutional limitations upon governmental authority is quite comprehensive in the Federal Republic and it is vigorously enforced, in a manner reminiscent of the zenith of "substantive due process" in American constitutional history before 1937, through an elaborate system of judicial review of legislative and administrative action. [14]

Powerful as judicial enforcement may be, the effectiveness of constitutional limitations can only be appreciated if one also looks at the ideological *cordon sanitaire* surrounding them. In an intensely legalistic political culture in which constitutional interpretation is continuously influenced (and revitalized) by the political issues of the day and in which political issues are very often formulated in constitutional-law terms, this twilight zone between 'hard core' constitutional law and outright partisan ideology has achieved a peculiar significance. Here, symbolic issues are likely to dominate the discussion of policy initiatives and, given their primarily defensive character, they will most often be used to delegitimate rather than to support active policy-making.

Perhaps most powerful in the arsenal of para-constitutional rethoric is the concept of the 'social market economy' which, canonized by the 'economic miracle' of the fifties, has translated

15

the propositions of neo-classical economics into normative standards to which all parties are paying much more than lip-service. [15] Thus, measures of economic policy are first judged not by their effectiveness but by the criterion of their 'market conformity', with the consequence that price controls are still regarded as unacceptable, rent controls have been abolished, wages, collective bargaining, and strikes are beyond governmental regulation, and even foreign exchange controls seemed so abhorrent that Professor Schiller, the powerful Minister of Finance and Economic Affairs, would rather resign from the cabinet and eventually leave his party in 1972, than accept some mild curbs on international currency speculation. Similarly, much of the current debate over industrial policy in West Germany does not focus on the effectiveness of specific measures, but remains on the level of an ideological debate over either the abstract necessity or the equally abstract illegitimacy of investment controls.

Similar ideological norms help to support the primacy of (state subsidized) private and denominational organizations in the operation of many charitable, social welfare, and educational services. In another area, the 'privacy of the doctor-patient relationship' has become a principle that effectively impedes the expansion of public health services, and the difficulties of an active research policy which were described in the preceding section are considerably increased by the widespread acceptance of self-serving interpretations of the 'freedom of research' by the spokesmen for the academic community.

It is unlikely that these and similar ideological interpretations would stand the test of constitutional litigation. Still, their deterrent effect in the political process does depend upon their close association with the authority and legitimacy of the constitution. The effectiveness of such principles in the twilight zone of constitutional interpretation is not primarily measured by the number or importance of government policies that have been declared unconstitutional by the courts. It should be measured in the terms of their ability to prevent or impede the presentation and discussion of a whole range of potential policy alternatives through a 'mobilization of bias' which discredits certain issues as such and relegates them to the area of 'non-decisions'. [16] Under such conditions, the authority of the political system is in effect more narrowly defined than an analysis of constitutional law would suggest. It is obvious that active policy-making should suffer more from such restraints than would a pattern of reactive, incremental policy-making.

16

3.2 Institutional differentiation and policy interpenetration

Along a second dimension the notion of organizational prerequisites refers to the capacity of the political system to employ its aggregate powers in active policy-making processes. As in all constitutional democracies, governmental power in the Federal Republic is institutionally differentiated to a considerable degree. From the perspective of national policy-making, the vertical division of powers between local governments, state governments, and the federal government does present a major organizational problem because West German federalism has a number of unique features which affect policy-making capacities at all levels of government.

At present, the federal system consists of the federal government and ten states (not counting West Berlin) which vary in population from Bremen with about 700.000 inhabitants to North-Rhine-Westphalia with more than 17 million inhabitants, and in wealth from the Saar with a gross domestic product per capita of DM 7.090,-- to Hamburg with a GDP per capita of DM 15.543,-- in 1968. At the local level, there were in 1969 more than 23.000 local government units in the Federal Republic, of which fully 44% had less than 500 inhabitants, and more than 67% had less than 1,000 inhabitants. [17] The number of local units, however, is rapidly decreasing as a consequence of local government reform creating larger units with a minimum size of about 5.000 inhabitants.

Compared to other federal systems, the Federal Republic is characterized by a peculiar and intensive interpenetration of the policy-making processes of the three levels of government. In the field of legislation, there is a clear preponderance of federal powers with a very limited area of exclusive state jurisdiction, mainly in the fields of education and of local government organization. Similarly, state autonomy in the field of taxation is extremely restricted; the major revenues of the states depend on taxes whose levels are determined by federal legislation and whose proceeds are constitutionally or by statute allocated to the states. But, while the federal government is paramount in legislation and taxation, the states do participate in the exercise of these federal powers through their representation in the *Bundesrat*. Its approval is needed for all legislation directly affecting state interests, and its veto in other matters can be overwritten only by qualified majorities of the First Chamber, the *Bundestag*. In actual practice, the

17

Bundesrat does exercise an effective veto over all important domestic legislation including, of course, taxation. [18] On the other hand, the states are paramount in the field of administration. The implementation of federal statutes is generally left to the states, and the federal government maintains its own administrative services only in a very limited number of areas like the military, the postal service and the national railroad system. The federal government (with the approval of the *Bundesrat*) may issue general regulations governing the administration of federal statutes, but its authority to control individual decisions remains extremely limited. The relationship between the federal government and the states is, therefore, one of mutual dependence in which federal legislation requires the consent of the states, and, for its implementation, the collaboration of state administration, while the states are limited in their legislative authority and depend upon federal legislation for their own revenue.

The same pattern is roughly repeated between the states and local governments. The autonomous jurisdiction of municipalities is restricted, but again, local government units are used as administrative agencies for the implementation of state administrative functions (including those determined by federal legislation). While local governments have a tax base of their own, they have become increasingly dependent upon general or conditional financial grants from the states and from the federal government. [19] And even though there is no formal representation of local governments in state decision processes, the frequent election of mayors as deputies to the state parliaments has provided an effective functional equivalent. As a consequence, there are very few areas, where policy can be determined *and* implemented exclusively at one level of government. Formally or informally, two or even three levels are usually involved in the making and execution of any decision.

The interpenetration of policy levels has further increased through the evolution of a peculiar modality of 'cooperative federalism' called *Gemeinschaftsaufgaben* (joint programs). Building upon a tradition of conditional federal grants to the states, legalized by constitutional amendment in 1969, *Gemeinschaftsaufgaben* require joint, federal-state planning and financing of policies in the areas of university construction, big science, regional economic policy, agricultural policy, housing, urban renewal, local transportation, and hospital construction. In all these areas, policies can only be adopted with the consent of both, the federal

18

government and the participating states. [20] Given frequent conflicts of interest between the two levels of government which are intensified by political conflict between Social-Liberal and Christian Democratic governments, consensus is hard to achieve and fragile. For organizational reasons, therefore, policy interpenetration would require powerful (and highly improbable) consensus-building mechanisms between the levels of government. If they are unavailable, the result must be either political deadlock and mutual obstruction or a systemic tendency toward conflict reduction through policies converging on the lowest common political denominator. For active policy-making, both alternatives seem equally unattractive.

In the German political and constitutional discussion, a growing dissatisfaction with the consequences of the prevailing pattern of policy interpenetration has led to demands for a redistribution of fiscal revenues which would permit state and local governments to pursue their own policies with their own resources. [21] Similar hopes are associated with plans for a territorial reorganization of the Federal Republic which would create five or six states that are more nearly equal in size, population, and economic and fiscal potential. [22] By thus eliminating small and financially weak states (which are particularly dependent upon federal grants), the proponents also hope to reduce the need for and, eventually, the actual extent of policy-interpenetration between the federal and state levels.

While such proposals, whose implementation seems politically quite uncertain, might help to reduce the need for joint policy-making, they would surely not eliminate it. Quite apart from the insufficiency of fiscal resources at the state and local levels, or from overlapping jurisdictions, the need arises from the substantive interdependence of federal, state and local policies. Local housing and state education programs are necessarily affected by federal immigration policies; local and state industrial policies depend upon fiscal, monetary, trade and sectoral policies at the federal level; both the causes and the solutions of local transportation problems are determined by state and federal highway and railroad policies; and any federal anti-cyclical policy or economic-growth policy depends upon, or may be frustrated by, state and local budgets and infrastructure investment patterns. Such interdependencies cannot be eliminated through any rearrangement of legislative, fiscal and administrative powers. They are the necessary consequence of growing differentiation and interdependence in the socio-economic as well as in the political system.

19

At this level of generality, the problems of differentiation and interdependence exist regardless of a two-level or three-level organization of government. Compared to a more centralized political system, like France, the more differentiated German political system probably achieves a greater degree of sensitivity to local and regional conditions and interests. It pays for the advantages of greater responsiveness through increased difficulties of vertical coordination. But while the trade-offs between the greater responsiveness of decentralized structures and the greater action potential of more centralized structures need much more study than they have received so far, the existing differences among highly developed western systems are probably differences in degree only. At any rate, we must assume that modern political systems need to achieve both, a degree of structural differentiation commensurate with their socio-economic environments and the ability to re-concert their differentiated action potentials in more complex, integrated patterns of active policy-making. One might say, however, that the Federal Republic is presently closer to the pole of over-differentation than most other developed Western systems, and that problems of inter-governmental coordination have, therefore, become increasingly important and difficult. It should be obvious that these difficulties, while organizational in origin, can hardly be resolved at the technical level of organizational and procedural arrangements alone. They are necessarily and intimately enmeshed in specifically political processes of conflict resolution and consensus building to which we turn in the next section. But even though dependent upon the macro-political context, the problems of differentiation and integration must also be dealt with internally through processes of coordination and concertation within the government, which will be described in chapter VIII, 3, below.

4. Political prerequisites

In this book, we start from a functional perspective, arguing that there exists a need for active policy-making and attempting to define the latter's prerequisites. This analytical perspective, however, should not lead to the mistaken belief that the political system is *in fact* characterized by the function we attribute to it. A realistic assessment of the way the political system operates must recognize that there are two basic—and often conflicting—

reference points of subsystem behavior: system needs and individual self-interest. Thus a political regime does not only aim to implement specific policies, it also wants to remain in power. These two goals may come into conflict. To the extent that the content of policy or the means chosen to secure its implementation cause discontent and provoke resistance, the pursuit of certain policy goals can threaten the political survival of a given government or even of the political system as a given set of institutional arrangements. The dependence on support is of course especially great in a parliamentary democracy, where it is even built into the constitution.

The crucial nature of support as a political resource has been widely recognized not only in political practice but also in political theory. [23] It is important, however, to distinguish between different kinds of support, namely:

- The general support enjoyed by a political system, expressed in the willingness to uphold the present institutional arrangement and abide by its rules;

- the general support enjoyed by a specific government, expressed in the willingness to return it to office in the next election;

- the support of specific policy decisions, expressed in the willingness to comply with them.

In the making of policy decisions, all three types of support are reference points which influence policy choice — not only because all of them are valid criteria of political rationality, but also because the various forms of support are interrelated, even though they can vary independently of each other. [24]

The strong dependence of the political system in a parliamentary democracy on support militates generally against policies which arouse resistance rather than agreement among the population. This poses a special problem for the pursuit of an active policy, which is less likely than a reactive policy to find support. Active policy-making which aims not merely at adaptation to, and compensation for, the effects of ongoing societal processes but at the direction and control of the processes themselves will not be Pareto optimal. Such policies will negatively affect important and politically influential social interests, at least in the short run, and will therefore typically be characterized by a negative rather than a positive balance of specific support and specific opposition.

Similarly, policy decisions which do not react to problems generally recognized as pressing but which attempt to prevent an anticipated *future* problem from arising, and which propose making large investments and imposing restrictions on individual action to this end, will not find support very easily. By and large, as policy moves from the "reactive" pole of the continuum toward the "active" pole it therefore tends increasingly to create conflicts between the political system and its environment. For an active policy, support is therefore not only a crucial but a critically scarce resource. We shall first consider briefly the existing level of supply or relative scarcity of general support in the Federal Republic. Later on we will discuss how considerations of support influence policy choices and what the political system can do to activate the resolution of conflicts and the mobilization of support.

4.1 General system support

It is understandable from German history that both foreign as well as German observers have often expressed doubts about the support which the system of parliamentary democracy actually enjoys in the Federal Republic. In the analysis of Almond and Verba, for instance, the Federal Republic appeared to be characterized by low system support in spite of a relatively high level of satisfaction with specific policy outputs. [25] Doubts as to the stability of the democratic political system were intensified when, as a consequence of the first economic recession in 1966/67, opposition against the political system became manifest in votes for the NPD, a right-fringe extremist party which, in some state parliaments, conquered between 8% and 10% of the seats. [26] In the meantime, the NPD which never entered the federal parliament has also lost all its representatives in the states. In federal and state legislatures, only Social Democrats, Christian Democrats, and Free Democrats can now be found, all of which fully support the existing political system.

During the same period, however, an 'extraparliamentary opposition' movement appeared on the left of the political spectrum. Overlapping with the student rebellion, this movement turned primarily against the formation of the 'Grand Coalition' of Christian Democrats and Social Democrats in late 1966 and against the emergency power amendments to the constitution, which this coalition adopted over the feeble parliamentary opposition of the

22

Free Democrats. In its self-perception, this was a movement in defense of the democratic political system; but on its left wing radical marxist and anarchist groups moved in fact toward a fundamental opposition against state and society. After the formation of the Social-Liberal coalition in 1969, the extraparliamentary opposition gradually disppeared as a mass movement. On its left fringe, a hard core of anarchists entered into a phase of highly publicized, but eventually abortive terrorism; sizeable segments of the intellectual opposition to the system have found shelter in the universities and the educational system; others have begun to work within political parties and have, in the meantime, gained substantial political power by strengthening the left wing of both the Free Democrats and the Social Democrats. But the great majority of the followers of the opposition movement seem to have returned to a lower level of political activity, or even to political apathy. Thus, the West German political system, while not unchallenged, has not been confronted with a serious loss of generalized system support over the last years and may even have gained in democratic stability during the ten years that have elapsed since the Almond and Verba study.

One of the most powerful stabilizing mechanisms of multiparty democracies (as distinguished from totalitarian one-party systems) is the differentiation of political system and governing parties. If dissatisfaction with specific policies accumulates, this need not affect general system support, because such dissatisfaction can be vented in the next election by not returning the present government to office. Such change of governments through the ballot need not affect the basic support of the system. This mechanism is underestimated in neo-marxist analyses which predict that the cumulative dissatisfaction of the population with the policy performance of the system will by itself develop into a pre-revolutionary situation. Elections may of course loose some of their stabilizing effect if the chance to sway the ruling majority is minimal or if even a change of government leads no longer to a visible change in policy. But this is not typical of the German situation, at least not since the Christian Democrats lost their control of the government in the 1969 election.

4.2 Governmental support

In a competitive situation, any party or coalition in power must be sensitive to the danger of loosing political support. This danger is indeed more real than the danger of a loss of general system support, because it is easier for the disaffected citizen to change his party allegiance and vote for the opposition party than to engage in revolutionary activity to overthrow the system. With the erosion of traditional political loyalties, significant and increasing proportions of voters are in fact changing their party allegiance from one election to the next. [27]

Considerations of support influence policy decisions particularly where a narrow electoral majority signifies a low level of general support for the government and the danger of not returning to office after the next election seems real. Where its political survival is not at stake, the government in its choice of policies could afford to pay attention primarily to the chances of implementation, where the specific support which a given policy receives is only one among several factors. Compliance can also be secured on the basis of the government's legitimacy, it can be conceded in repayment for other benefits received, it can directly be bargained for, or it can be enforced by legal means such as the threat of fines or the loss of former rights or privileges. Where implementation is the main problem, the balance of satisfaction and dissatisfaction associated with a given policy is at any rate not the main criterion of choice between alternatives.

This changes radically when considerations of political survival become dominant. Under this condition the government is compelled to consider first and foremost the reactions of the electorate to its policy decisions. But the anticipation of future voter reactions to present policy decisions is extremely difficult. For one thing the voter must aggregate his separate reactions to separate policy decisions in one ballot, and it is difficult to anticipate the relative importance of any one of his reactions for his final decision. Moreover a given policy decision can have quite different effects on voting behavior, depending on whether it is the evaluation of policy content or the subsequent impact of the implemented policy to which the voters primarily react at the time of the next election. Voter reactions to policy impact are probably more diffuse; at any rate they take more time to become effective and they are even more difficult to predict than immediate voter reactions to an announced policy decision. This probably makes for a tendency to neglect long-term policy impact in favor of the anticipated immediate reaction to policy content in calculating the effects of a specific policy decision on voting behavior. When they are hard pressed not to loose popular support, politicians more-

24

over seem to choose a minimax strategy in predicting voter behavior. To be on the safe side, they assume that every group of voters which is objectively disadvantaged by a particular policy will be (1) fully aware of this disadvantage and will (2) react to it negatively at the time of the next election. This criterion of decision must obviously operate against the formulation of an active policy which tends to provoke more immediate dissatisfactions than a reactive one.

Long-range reform strategies are politically unattractive also for an additional reason. If the positive effect of a policy will become felt only in a later legislative period, while the decision as such may not be very popular at present, the government which makes this decision may well invest in an enterprise of which the opposition will earn the profit. By increasing the dependence of governments on popular support, multi-party democracy thus generates pressures to maximize short-term success.

These various pressures are compounded where the government is formed by a coalition, because in coalition governments the individual parties will make their separate calculations of support. Depending upon the location of their supporters in the electorate their chances to gain from a specific policy decision will be different. But as the veto of one coalition party is usually enough to block a proposal, the expectations of political loss of all coalition parties will cumulate rather than neutralize each other. As a consequence, coalition governments tend to avoid political risks to a much higher degree than single-party governments.

The conditions just described in abstract terms have existed throughout the history of the Federal Republic with the exception of four years of an absolute Christian-Democratic majority from 1953-1957; they were most pronounced during the legislative period 1969-1972. The government coalition started in 1969 with a very narrow parliamentary majority of 12 deputies, of whom 3 deserted to the opposition within the first year of the legislative period, cutting the majority down to 6. [28] Nevertheless, the government coalition pursued a highly controversial policy toward East Germany, which eventually reduced its parliamentary majority to zero. On top of this, the coalition was losing support through its inability to stop inflation which, during the 1969 election, had been one of its major campaign themes and which remained one of the most sensitive issues of German politics. At the same time the coalition was confronted both by the fears and by the hopes raised by its program of 'domestic reforms'. In addition, both coalition parties were relying for support on different population groups, the Social Democrats primarily upon the working class and critical intellectuals, the Free Democrats mainly upon artisans, farmers and the new middle class of academically trained employees. Under such conditions, the actual balance of support and opposition had to become an extremely narrow constraint of policy proposals during the last parliamentary term. While the safe parliamentary majority which the coalition gained in the premature election of 1972 decreased this pressure noticeably, the basic situation described above still remains and with it the need to make careful calculations of support in the choice of policies.

We have emphasized the restrictive effect which the need to gain sufficient popular support can have on policy decisions, especially where politicians base their anticipation of popular reactions on highly simplified and pessimistic "safe" assumptions. But this does not mean that a government can do in fact nothing else but adjust its policy choices to the given reaction tendencies of social groups, and advance only such programs as will receive a favorable evaluation in terms of the satisfaction of fixed demands. This is a view of politics which may result from an exchange theory of political behavior such as Ilchman and Uphoff have developed, neglecting the fact that popular expectations, demands, and policy evaluations are subject to processes of social definition and situational interpretation. Political discontent is not simply a reflex of real situations, but depends on processes of opinion formation which can at least partly be manipulated by the political system. To put it crudely: to gain support the government need not give people what they ask for, if it can persuade them of what they should want and can legitimately expect to get.

More precisely, the government can adopt two strategies which both extend its sphere of action. It can, first, secure for itself a capital of general support which does not repay actual services rendered or goods delivered, but is given in response to a skillful manipulation of symbols, e.g. by building up the belief in the historical mission or charismatic qualities of a political leader. Secondly it can influence the expectations and evaluations of citizens regarding policy choices, for instance by fostering the feeling of a state of impending national emergency, in this way revising the level of aspiration downward and creating a willingness to make sacrifices. Similarly the feeling of a state of crisis can be used by astute politicians to introduce reforms or redefine financial priorities without meeting with the opposition that otherwise would have arisen. This happened in the Federal Republic in the case of the so-called educational crisis and later in the case of the "environmental crisis". When it becomes clear that in spite of the efforts made to overcome a given crisis, much of the original problem remains unresolved, political impression management can make use of the fact of issue competition to prevent the cumulative growth of dissatisfaction by diverting public attention to a new problem area. Thus, before the energy crisis became real enough in the winter of 1973/74, its predicted approach had already been used to play down the "environmental crisis" which had come to a first culmination point, [29] giving rise to many demands for interventions and improvements which are difficult to fulfill. To the extent that politicians realize the potential influence of political impression management on governmental support, their use of such strategies will diminish their dependence on the popular evaluation of program content, thus strengthening the political system's autonomy vis-à-vis its environment.

We may conclude that the ability of the political system to overcome resistance, to resolve conflicts induced by policy, and to gain support is of decisive importance for the development of an active policy. Since political support is an essential prerequisite, no reforms aiming to improve the capacity of the political system to develop an active policy will be successful which do not increase the capacity of the system to mobilize support in the same measure in which such a policy is likely to increase opposition.

4.3 Action consensus

Since the political system is internally differentiated it does not behave like an unitary actor in making policy choices. Policy proposals must first of all find consensus within the political action system, which was defined above as that subset of the political system which effectively determines policy decisions. As in the case of external support, the availability of action consensus within the political system should be seen in a dynamic perspective as the result of two critical variables, the level of disagreement or conflict on the one hand and the capability to resolve conflict and achieve consensus on the other hand.

Conflicts over policy choices arise within the political action system partly by way of a projection, or internalization, of conflicting demands in the socio-economic environment. Various sectors of the environment have their institutionalized spokesmen within the action system. Thus, the political parties, but also the various ministries represent different social groups and their interests within the action system. Where the demands of these different social groups within the environment are conflicting, conflicts over policy content will also arise within the political action system, both where such conflict grows out of the competition for scarce resources and where it results from an incompatibility of goals. These conflicts are superimposed upon and often reinforce conflicts which arise within the action system from a structurally determined difference in perspective of the various participants.

The participants within the political action system may not only pursue different policy goals. In addition each of them is individually faced with a problem of political survival or organizational self-maintenance, which is distinct from the survival of the government and the survival of the political system as such. This has been pointed out already with regard to coalition parties forming one government, but it similarly holds for the other participants in the action system: the federal ministries, the state governments, the parliamentary parties — down to the very individuals who compose these groups. Individual, positional and organizational interests lead to conflicts over scarce resources and competition for power, public attention, and success. These conflicts can become linked with conflicts over policy content in a given issue, thus reinforcing the latter. But differences of political opinion can also be neutralized by the exigencies of political survival where the fate of one participant is closely linked with that of another, a situation in which the Social Democrats often found themselves vis-à-vis the Free Democrats since 1969.

The goal of individual political survival also brings considerations of external support to bear upon the achievement of internal action consensus. Participants in the action system who have reason to fear a negative reaction of certain groups of voters will agree to a policy proposal only if they think it will be positively evaluated by these groups. A policy thus tends to become controversial within the action system to the extent that its adoption affects the political survival of the participants differently, which is especially true of proposals for an active policy. An active policy will therefore not only find external support less easily than a reactive policy, but will — partly for this reason — also find it more difficult to achieve action consensus within the political system.

Other things being equal, the achievement of action consensus grows also more difficult as a given decision depends on the agreement of an increasing number of participants. Thus, in the Federal Republic where the consent or cooperation of the states is needed for most national policies, the probability of conflict within the action system is higher than in a more centralized political system.

The main lines of conflict within the political action system of the Federal Republic are (1) conflicts within the government, (2) conflicts between the federal government and the states, and (3) conflicts within parliament, i.e. between the different party groups. There is little conflict between the federal government and parliament, because according to the constitution the cabinet is chosen by the parliamentary majority and can be considered the executive of the majority party or ruling coalition.

We shall deal with conflicts arising within the government in general and the federal bureaucracy in particular in chapter VIII. Conflicts between the federal government and the states involve questions of formal competence, but also questions of policy content. Some national policies do not affect all states in the same way and are opposed by those who feel disadvantaged. Differences of political opinion also occur because at least part of the states are ruled by other parties or coalitions than that of the federal government. Often both types of conflict are linked in an issue, the question of formal competence being only raised to ward off a policy decision found objectionable on substantive grounds. But the issue of formal competence is also raised independently of concrete policy issues, because the states try to defend their authority and resources against the necessarily centralistic implications of an active policy pursued by the federal government.

Conflicts within parliament are mainly about policy content. In most of these conflicts power motives and policy convictions are inextricably intertwined, since the political survival needs of individuals and party groups attach themselves to substantive policy issues.

To achieve action consensus in the face of such manifold conflicts the action system must have a sufficiently large capacity for conflict resolution. The crucial importance of this factor has been neglected by recent developments in the policy sciences which have primarily focused upon the efficiency of resource allocation, informational and technological rationality, and organizational coordination. [30] We shall deal with the capacity for conflict resolution at the level of the federal government and the federal bureaucracy in chapter IX. Here some very general remarks about strategies of conflict resolution along the other lines of conflict within the Federal Republic's political action system must suffice.

Authoritative decision serves not at all to resolve conflicts between party groups in parliament, and very little to achieve action consensus between the federal government and the states, since these action partners stand neither in a relationship of hierarchical authority to each other, nor is there a common hierarchical authority to which they might appeal — except in the case of constitutional-law disputes. Persuasion and the appeal to common goals are limited in their effects as strategies for achieving action consensus by the ideological differences between the political parties, which in the Federal Republic are — today even less than it might have appeared only five years ago — anything but mere platform parties which are only marginally differentiated in their appeals. This limitation holds for conflicts within parliament as well as for conflicts between the federal government and the states, which are often governed by different parties or coalitions. Occasionally it is possible to change the relevant action system by moving an issue from one arena with one set of participants to another where agreement may be easier to achieve. Thus appeals from parliamentary conflict to a 'coalition committee' may significantly change the probability of conflict resolution. In general, however, the action system is constitutionally or legally fixed and cannot be changed at will. The main strategy for achieving action consensus is therefore bargaining in all of its ways and variants, including the skillful alignment of coalitions.

From the preceding analysis it appears that while the situation with regard to the supply of external support and internal action consensus in the Federal Republic is not particularly critical, a shift towards a more active policy would probably increase conflict rather quickly to that level where it overstrains the existing capacity for conflict resolution. The political prerequisites of active policy-making are at present probably not less fulfilled or in shorter supply than the prerequisites discussed in the preceding sections, but it may be more difficult to increase support and consensus without basic changes in the socio-economic structure and the political constitution of the Federal Republic than it would be to increase, for instance, the level of information.

Chapter III

THE STRUCTURE OF THE FEDERAL ACTION SYSTEM

After the more abstract discussions of prerequisites of active policy-making, we now turn to a summary description of the main components of the federal action system which was defined above as that part of the political system within which policy decisions are effectively determined. It concludes the party organizations of the majority coalition and their parliamentary parties, parliament and its committees, the *Bundesrat*, the cabinet, the Chancellor's Office, and the ministerial departments. While this action system will respond to external inputs and constraints, federal policies must be processed and adopted within the institutions included here. But even though all of them may contribute to federal policy-making, their contributions do in fact vary considerably in scope and effective weight in the policy process. Thus, the ability of the federal action system to develop and adopt active policies will depend to different degrees upon the structural conditions within its several institutional sub-systems.

1. Political party organizations

Compared to the fifties and sixties, the role of political party organizations in federal policy-making has considerably increased during the period of the social-liberal coalition to which our study primarily refers. [1] But this change was not entirely abrupt, and much of it can be attributed to the entrance of the Social Democratic Party (SPD) into the governing coalition as a junior partner in 1966, and as the dominant group since 1969. While the Christian Democrats (CDU/CSU) had treated policy-making, and domestic policies in particular, as primarily government and parliamentary business during their time in power [2], the Social Democrats have throughout their history of more than 110 years remained a highly ideological and strongly programmatic organization. [3] As an opposition party throughout most of their history, they had no opportunity to develop a strong government wing, and their parliamentary party was, on the whole, politically subservient to the general party organization and its political strategies and programs.

The situation changed somewhat when, in the late fifties and early sixties, the party reacted to disastrous electoral defeats by discarding much of its dogmatic ideology in favor of a more flexible, pragmatic platform. This movement, culminating in the adoption of the *Godesberg Program* in 1959, had been led by the parliamentary party pursuing a strategy that minimized its disagreement with the main lines of government policy, especially in the areas of defence, European integration and economic policy, in order to move close enough to the political center to become an acceptable choice for middle class voters. [4] This strategy finally paid off when, in the government crisis of later 1966, the Christian Democrats were forced to accept the SPD as a partner in the 'Grand Coalition' which was replaced by the Social-Liberal Coalition after the elections of 1969.

For the Social Democratic party, however, the Grand Coalition was a traumatic episode. It found itself in government together with the Christian Democrats whom they had fought at every political turn since 1949, and who seemed to exploit the coalition as a mere expedient for continuing their previous policies. Worse yet, the Social Democrats seemed to lack specific programmatic goals of their own that could produce significant changes in government policy.

At the same time, the party membership reacted to the fundamentalist challenge of the 'extra-parliamentary opposition' with an unexpected revival of ideological and programmatic discussion. This trend continued when the 'new left' began to integrate into the party, joining forces with older leftist groups which had never accepted the pragmatism of the sixties. As the situation in government remained unsatisfactory after 1969, with a narrow majority, a tight fiscal situation and the veto power of the Free Democrats severely limiting the opportunities for Social Democratic reform policies, the party intensified its internal discussion. In addition to the regular biennial party conventions at the federal and state levels, extraordinary conventions and a series of party conferences dealt with such substantive policy areas as tax reform, education reform, or the reform of real estate law. As a culmination of this movement, the 1970 national convention requested the preparation of a 'long-range program for societal policy which must be concrete and quantified'. The publication of a draft 'frame of orientation for 1973-1985' in the summer of 1972 was followed by the most wide-ranging and sophisticated programmatic debate the party had experienced since the adoption of the *Godesberg Program*, and the convention of 1973, while highly critical of the draft, voted for the continuation of long-range policy planning at the party level.

It remains to be seen whether further work on the program will lead to effective and financially realistic policy commitments of the Social Democratic Party over a wide range of government policy areas. Until now at least, the intensified programmatic discussion has focussed on a few policy areas and has rarely reached that degree of concreteness and financial realism which would have permitted its direct translation into government policy. Furthermore, while the Free Democrats have also intensified their programmatic commitments in their party conventions, they have tended to do so primarily in those areas like tax reform, or codetermination in industry, or real estate law, where the interests of their clientele groups and, consequently, their party goals differed most from Social Democratic policies. As a consequence, the important policy comprises still have to be worked out within the government coalition, in the executive branch and in parliament. Party organizations have become relatively more important in a number of policy areas, but they have not yet gained a controlling influence over policy formation as a whole.

2. Parliamentary party groups

Unlike the general party organizations, the parliamentary parties are, of course, very intimately involved in the process of government policy-making. This was true to an extreme degree under the conditions of the Grand Coalition with its uneasy alignment of two large groups in direct competition with each other. During that period, neither parliamentary group would uncritically accept those government proposals which emerged from ministries held by the other party. Thus, all major policy initiatives had to pass through elaborate procedures of scrutiny, 'politicking', bargaining and consensus building between the parliamentary groups of the majority before their adoption could be assured. During this period, the positions of the parliamentary leaders of both major parties, Rainer Barzel and Helmut Schmidt, developed into centers of political power far exceeding their usual importance in parliamentary systems and almost on a level with the power of the chancellorship.

While the confrontation between a narrow governing majority and a powerful and vigorous opposition, after 1969, did reduce the relative political importance of the parliamentary parties, they have nevertheless remained influential. That their loyalty could not be taken for granted was demonstrated within a few months of the 1969 election, when the parliamentary party of the SPD vetoed a tax surcharge that the government had proposed as a measure to reduce consumer demand in its fight against inflation. With the continuing erosion of its parliamentary support, the government could have been brought down by the desertion of one or two of its deputies on any single issue and, therefore, had to fully consult its parliamentary parties long before any legislative initiative was brought to a vote.

On the whole, however, the role of parliamentary parties in policy-making remains limited. They respond to early information about governmental policy proposals, and their criticism will definitely influence and change the content of such proposals, but they will hardly embarrass the government — as the opposition will often try to do — by introducing their own legislative initiatives when the government is active in a particular field. But of course, opposition initiatives are rarely successful in a parliamentary system. Thus, the active involvement of the parliamentary parties does not basically detract from the policy-making responsibility of the government in power. [5]

3. Parliament and parliamentary committees

If the parliamentary parties of the majority are not often initiators of major policy ventures, that is even more true of the institutional parliament as a whole. It may react to and modify government proposals, but it rarely will determine the substance and content of policy initiatives. In a parliamentary system, this is certainly true of the plenary sessions of parliament, where the government majority and the opposition will publicly debate, but not substantively change pre-determined policy positions. In this sense, plenary sessions and debates belong to the symbolic or, to use Bagehot's phrase, the 'dignified parts of the constitution', rather than to the effective policy-making process.

If in its plenary sessions the *Bundestag* follows the pattern of all parliamentary systems, the power of its committees seems to correspond more nearly to that of the American Congress. This is not merely true of the budget committee which tightly controls all appropriations, but also of the legislative committees whose jurisdiction closely corresponds to the ministerial organization. The mere fact that even during the last years of extreme confrontation the great majority of all statutes were passed unanimously or with majorities far exceeding the voting strength of the coalition, presupposes substantial opportunities for the opposition to participate in policy-making and to influence the content of legislation. This opportunity is offered through the committee structure where, in the absence of publicity and in a relatively non-political atmosphere, specialists and interest-group representatives from all parties collaborate in the technical improvement and modification of legislative proposals.

Parliamentary committees had reached the height of their power during the Grand Coalition, when they were often able to block or change substantially legislative proposals that had been introduced by the government. The very fact that the government was formally supported by an overwhelming parliamentary majority also meant that none of its proposals could automatically count on the loyalty of a disciplined majority, and that substantive policy compromises which had not been reached at the ministerial level were in fact worked out in parliamentary committees. In the German pattern, this was an unusual situation which overemphasized the regular function of parliament and its committees in the policy-making process. Committees have, however, remained unusually powerful even after the termination of the Grand Coalition in 1969. The reason lies in the peculiar combination of political majorities in parliament and in the *Bundesrat*. While the Social-Liberal coalition after 1969 was supported first by a narrow and then by a solid majority of *Bundestag* deputies, the Christian-Democrats continued to control a narrow majority of the state votes in the *Bundesrat*. In parliamentary committees, therefore, the opposition members could and did use the leverage of a potential *Bundesrat* veto in order to bargain for substantial modifications of coalition initiatives. The game, which was often played with great tactical skill, has helped to perpetuate some decision-making patterns of the Grand Coalition, and it is largely responsible for the ambiguities in the style of national politics which combine increasingly ideological public confrontations between government and opposition with much hard-headed bargaining and pragmatic compromise behind the closed doors of parliamentary committees.

Impressive as the power of parliamentary committees may have been during the last years, one should still be careful with generalization. Much of this power seems to have depended upon extraordinary circumstances — first the Grand Coalition and then the indirect, but effective veto of the parliamentary opposition through its influence upon *Bundesrat* votes. Under both circumstances, the power of committees might be regarded as borrowed power which might quickly erode when the overall political constellation should change back toward parallel, but narrow, political majorities in both houses of the legislature. Still, an elaborate committee structure with the most influencial parliamentarians of all parties as chairman of the important committees will assure the West German parliament of a degree of substantive influence in policy processes that is not found in the classical parliamentary systems. In this respect, the West German legislature seems closer in power to the American Congress than to its counterparts in parliamentary forms of government. [6]

4. Bundesrat

Formally and in actual practice, the involvement of the second chamber, the *Bundesrat*, in federal policy-making is considerable. Even among federal systems which provide for the representation of state interests at the national level, this is a unique institution in which state governments are directly represented — usually through their prime ministers and cabinet members. Constitutionally, the consent of the *Bundesrat* is needed for certain categories of federal legislation directly affecting state finances and the state administration of federal statutes, while in all other instances its veto may be overridden by qualified parliamentary majorities. But the limited categories of 'consent legislation' have been so expanded by interpretation and by a series of constitutional admendments that in actual practice the *Bundesrat* does possess an effective veto over most important domestic legislation.

36

Generally, the second chamber has exercised its veto primarily in defense of specific state interests and with a view to improving the technical quality of legislation from the point of view of state administration which is mostly responsible for its implementation. It has rarely taken the legislative initiative, and it has rarely focussed directly upon the political aspects of federal policy. [7] The pattern changed considerably, however, after 1969 when, for the first time in the history of the Federal Republic, the *Bundesrat* came under the political control of the parliamentary opposition. Thereafter, the Christian Democratic majority in the *Bundesrat* focussed its opposition on the political substance of the legislative program that the Social-Liberal coalition had passed in the *Bundestag*, and the resulting compromises were clearly determined by party-political bargaining. [8]

At first, the uncertainty of the Social-Liberal parliamentary majority and the hope of jolting it through a series of legislative defeats may have contributed to the new political pattern which was in manifest conflict with past practice and with the constitutional role that the *Bundesrat* had defined for itself. The pattern continues, however, now that the Social-Liberal majority in parliament is quite secure, so that the active political opposition of the *Bundesrat* must be considered a stable feature of the political system as long as the present distribution of partisan majorities will continue. The relatively bureaucratic, a-political role that the *Bundesrat* had defined for itself during the first twenty years of its history thus seems to have depended primarily upon the existence of parallel partisan majorities in both houses. Even so, however, the *Bundesrat* remains primarily a veto power in the policy-making process. It did not, and probably cannot, develop into a major center of active policy initiative.

That the center of policy initiative is occupied by the executive branch of government had become a truism in Germany as elsewhere. If the statistical score seems less than impressive in this respect, [9] three factors should be kept in mind: Legislative initiatives by members of parliament often deal with minor matters that may be functionally equivalent to the private bills in the American Congress. Secondly, opposition initiatives on major matters may be frequent, but they are not often successful and should be interpreted more as appeals to public opinion than as attempts at effective policy-making. Thirdly, legislative initiatives by the parliamentary majority are often government initiatives in disguise. This happens frequently with very urgent bills for which the government wishes to avoid the three-week delay in the *Bundesrat* to which government bills (but not private-member bills) are subject before deliberations in parliament may begin. Thus, even though parliament and the *Bundesrat* seem more influential in Germany than in other parliamentary systems, it is still fair to say ✶ that active policy-making is dominated by the executive branch.

Most critics of modern parliamentarism seem content to leave it at that, lumping together the ministerial bureaucracy, the Chancellor's Office, the ministers and the chancellor in one aggregate bureaucratic-executive complex which they see as nearly omnipotent vis-à-vis a feeble and subservient legislature. Here as elsewhere, however, the more interesting questions can only be asked if one looks at the separate components of such over-aggregated categories. In this overview, we will follow the constitutional differentiation which allocates separate functions to the chancellor, the cabinet and the individual ministers.

5. The chancellor

By the law of the constitution, the chancellor is the only member of government directly responsible to parliament. He needs an absolute majority for his election, and he can only be ousted from office if parliament elects a successor — again by absolute majority. This provision, which was intended to assure government stability in the face of negative coalitions was first tested in the parliamentary deadlock between the Social-Liberal coalition and the Christian-Democratic opposition in the spring of 1972, when it permitted a government that had lost its parliamentary majority to stay in office for another six months.

Apart from safeguarding the chancellor's tenure in office (which, of course, will not protect him against the loss of support within his own party or coalition, as both Adenauer and Erhard had to find out) the constitution provides him with three seemingly powerful instruments for determining or influencing substantive government policy: he unilaterally exercises the "organizing power" within the government, which permits him to create and abolish ministries and to define their jurisdictions without the need for parliamentary authorization or approval; [10] he unilaterally recommends the appointment and dismissal of ministers to the federal president; and he unilaterally issues general policy guidelines which are binding upon ministers.

In the exercise of these powers he is supported by the Chancellor's Office that has grown from a fairly small secretariat into a sizeable organization with over 400 employees, among them more than one hundred higher civil servants. [11] It is headed by the 'chief of the Chancellor's Office' who may be either a minister or a state secretary with civil-service status. Since 1967, there have been additional state secretaries (with parliamentary or civil-service status as will be explained below in chapter V, 4) in the Chancellor's Office, usually with special assignments such as Western- or Eastern-European policy coordination. Outside of the Chancellor's Office, but under the chancellor's authority, there is the Federal Press Office, headed by a state secretary of civil-service status who — like the chief of the Chancellor's Office — participates regularly in cabinet meetings.

5.1 Ministerial appointments

In spite of his impressive arsenal of constitutional powers and the bureaucratic machinery at his disposal, the influence of the chancellor on substantive government policy is fairly narrowly circumscribed in practice. In a coalition government, to begin with the most obvious constraint, the question of how many and which ministries should be held by which of the coalition parties is one of the chief subjects of coalition-building negotiations among all political parties after a general election and *before* the chancellor is elected in parliament. Of course, the future chancellor is an important participant in such bargaining processes, but he cannot unilaterally determine the outcome which will define the political base of his government. He depends upon the consensus not only of the coalition partners but also of his own party and its more powerful groups and individuals. In a parliamentary system, the important ministries will usually go to parliamentarians of high standing and influence, and in the Federal Republic additional political claims of the various state party organizations and of ideological and interest groupings within the parties have to be considered in the drafting of any cabinet list.

This internal pluralism was always most pronounced with the Christian Democrats whose cabinet lists with their delicate balance of catholics and protestants, northern, western, southern and refugee party organizations, big business, small business, agriculture and labour interests had to be appreciated as sublime works of the political art. But the Social Democrats have also lost much of their internal homogeneity and party discipline since they have come into power, and they are now confronted with almost the same problems of internal pluralistic balancing. Thus, even a chancellor who, like Willy Brandt in 1972, was the undisputed leader of his party and could claim most of the credit for a brilliant election victory, had to reserve the majority of ministrial assignments falling to his own party to candidates whose political claims he could not turn down without incurring prohibitive political costs. Even under the best of circumstances, the chancellor will be lucky if his unilateral preference should determine at least a few ministerial appointments.

5.2 Organizing power

The chancellor's 'organizing power' is limited by similar constraints. Coalition bargaining will, of course, extend to the question of which ministries should be created or abolished, and of how the lines of demarcation should be drawn between them. There is, however, an important difference between an incoming government and a government that was reelected. In the second case, when many ministers are reappointed to their old positions, departmental interests will combine with partisan positions in reducing the chancellor's freedom of choice. The boundaries of departmental jurisdiction are often the front lines of inter-departmental warfare with a long history of intense battles for small gains and losses of territory. Ministers who are reappointed to their former departments will not lightly agree to reorganization proposals that could be interpreted as their defeat in inter-departmental battle. New ministers, on the other hand, will be less identified with vested departmental interests and may be more able to accept major reorganization proposals.

5.3 Policy guidelines

The forces that limit the chancellor's powers of organization and of ministerial appointment also restrict his influence on substantive policy through issuing policy guidelines (*Richtlinien der Politik*) binding upon ministers. Unilateral directives will not work in the face of policy conflicts between the coalition parties, and they will not work very well if there are policy conflicts within the chancellor's own party. As a consequence, all chancellors have used this constitutional power very sparingly, and usually only for the purpose of coordinating ministries in some more technical and less political matters.

Of greater practical importance is the chancellor's influence on government policy through his *Regierungserklärung*. This declaration, delivered in parliament at the beginning of a new parliamentary term or after the formation of a new government, represents the political program to which the government wishes to commit itself. While not in a formal sense binding upon ministries, the declaration is nevertheless the yardstick by which the coalition parties, the opposition and the critical press will judge the political success or failure of a government. For that reason, such commitments usually enjoy high political priority within the ministries and also in the competition for funds in the annual budget.

The very political importance of the declaration will, however, also constrain its unilateral use by the chancellor. Coalition parties will not only bargain over ministerial appointments and jurisdictions but also over the government program that the chancellor will announce. In the case of policy conflict within the coalition, the chancellor's statement will carefully reflect the compromises that have been achieved. At the same time, the individual ministries will supply drafts describing their intentions and existing commitments, so that the chancellor's declaration is always in danger of being reduced to a mere compilation of current departmental policies.

The actual impact of the chancellor's policy declaration upon government policy will depend upon the concreteness and precision of its commitments, upon the mechanisms available for controlling its implementation and, of course, on subsequent events and developments, the most important of which has been the lack of funds. With regard to the first of these conditions, the chancellor is faced with a dilemma. If his commitments are very specific and concrete, it will be easier for the Chancellor's Office to supervise and control their implementation and, thus, to maximize his influence upon government policy. But, as the Social-Liberal coalition found out during its first term, a very specific government program will also be a very suggestive checklist of government failures, ready to be used by the opposition in its next election campaign. Thus, after some unpleasant experiences with the highly specific 1969 declaration, the chancellor's commitments after his reelection in 1972 were much more cautions and emphasized generalities rather than specifics.

Without specific policy guidelines, however, the supervisory and directive functions of the Chancellor's Office cannot be exercised systematically. While the Office will be able to monitor departmental policy processes, it can intervene effectively only within those areas that happen to attract the special attention of the chancellor himself or of other members of the leadership. That such policy influence can be far reaching and decisive, Willy Brandt and his state secretary Egon Bahr have demonstrated after 1969 in their successful conduct of West Germany's Eastern policy. But even though they have been able to rely upon the foreign-policy units of the Office, their influence remained personal rather than institutional, and it was limited by the working capacity and attention space of a few individuals.

During the same period, there has been no similar substantive influence of the chancellor upon domestic policy. This may change with shifts in the chancellor's attention, but there is surely no reason to assume that such influence could be exercised over the full range of domestic policy. The chancellor and the Chancellor's Office have not been able to achieve controlling influence over policy-making processes within the federal government. If such influence exists, it must therefore be exercised either by the Cabinet or by the individual ministries.

6. The cabinet

Under the constitution, the chancellor (unlike the American President) cannot issue specific directives and orders to ministers; his hierarchical authority is limited to general policy guidelines (*Richtlinien der Politik*). Under these guidelines each minister is independently responsible for the direction of affairs within the jurisdiction of his ministry. Disagreements among ministers are to be decided by the cabinet. Under the rules and procedures of the federal government, the cabinet as a collective body is also assigned all politically important decisions at the government level, including decisions on all legislative proposals, on the annual budget and the middle-range financial plan and their amendments, and even on all senior appointments within the bureaucracy down to the level of section heads.

But in spite of its impressive list of functions and its regular sessions at least once each week, the cabinet has not developed into a collective decision-making body that is in effective control of government policy. To some extent, this failure may simply be a function of its size: Since the foundation of the Federal Republic, the number of ministries has varied from a high of 19 in 1966/1969 to a low of 12 under the unusual conditions of a lame-duck government in the summer and fall of 1972. After the 1972 election, the cabinet again included the heads of 16 departments plus 2 ministers without portfolio and the chancellor. To these, the state secretaries of the Chancellor's Office and of the Federal Press Office should be added, while the parliamentary state secretaries of the ministries participate in cabinet meetings only in the absence of their ministers. At any rate, it would probably be difficult under any circumstances to forge an effective policy-making instrument out of an assembly of over 20 regular members. The difficulties are increased by the fact that the cabinet, as an institution, is without an adequate bureaucratic infrastructure. The Chancellor's Office, while it is sometimes defined as a cabinet secretariat, has never become fully effective as an instrument of the cabinet in its collective capacity. This seems to be less due to the chancellor's desire to monopolize the services of his office than to a lack of interest in, and even a distrust of, its functions on the part of cabinet members.

Ministers, at least after brief periods of initiation, have inevitably identified more with their roles as heads of departments than with their cabinet functions. It is as managers of their ministries and as promotors of department policies that they will eventually be judged successful or unsuccessful in professional and political opinion. As heads of departments they are able to utilize the services of a large and specialized policy-making bureaucracy, and they will be briefed on all other policy issues from a departmental point of view. As chief executives they must maintain the loyalty and motivation of the bureaucracies on which they depend by fighting vigorously for departmental policies and for departmental budgets. At the cabinet level, these basic structural conditions emphasize the parochial rather than the collective perspectives of ministers. As a consequence, cabinet members do not have a basic interest in strengthening the policy-making and policy-controlling capacities of the cabinet as a whole and of the Chancellor's Office which might only increase the danger of outside scrutiny and intervention in departmental policies even in cases when no other ministry should have reason to object.

Thus, the cabinet should be understood primarily as an assembly of heads of departments which must formally ratify important policy proposals originating from the departments. Its involvment in policy choices increases, however, in two situations: when interdepartmental conflicts have to be settled at the cabinet level, and when the budgetary process requires the resolution of conflicts over scarce resources. In both situations, conflicts need not necessarily be settled at the cabinet level. Interdepartmental disagreements on policy are usually worked out in bilateral or multilateral negotiations that assure that only agreed-upon proposals will reach the cabinet. In such bargaining processes the Chancellor's Office is usually involved in the role of a broker whose effectiveness depends on its access to backgroud information, the authority of the chancellor, and the expectation of the parties that the Office is not pursuing any specific policy goals of its own. Similarly, allocative conflicts in the annual budget are handled primarily by the Ministry of Finance so that, again, the cabinet is usually dealing with agreed-upon proposals.

In both instances, however, pre-cabinet processes of conflict reduction are not always effective. They tend to break down under pressure of time, or when policy conflicts involve strong outside interests which are represented within the government by separate ministries or by the coalition parties. The same may happen in the budgetary process when there are strong political forces pushing against budget ceilings imposed by the finance minister upon ministries or specific programs. Under such conditions, the substance of political choices will have to be determined by the cabinet on the basis of the political and institutional strength of the conflicting interests.

The creation of a larger number of cabinet committees in the last few years has not basically affected the pattern described here. With a few exceptions, these committees are usually not attended by ministeres or even state secretaries, but rather by higher ranking civil servants. Thus, they operate very much like other interministerial committees whose main function is to work out interdepartmental policy compromises below the political level. [12] The situation seems to be different in those few cabinet committees over which the chancellor himself presides and which are regularly attended by cabinet ministers. Thus, at least the "Finance Cabinet" and the "Defense Cabinet" — both with largely overlapping membership — have become something like an inner political core of the whole cabinet in which important policy choices can be discussed under less pressure from particularized departmental interests.

The situation is complicated, however, by the fact that both coalition parties have parliamentary leaders who must be included in any "inner circle" without regard to their cabinet position. During the Grand Coalition, this central locus of political power was semi-institutionalized in a coalition committee called the *Kressbronner Kreis* which included the chancellor (CDU), the vice-chancellor (SPD), the chairmen of both parliamentary parties, the secretaries general of the coalition parties, the minister of finance (CSU), the minister of economics (SPD) and one or two outstandingly influential politicians like, for instance, Herbert Wehner (SPD). The Social-Liberal coalition has not yet found it necessary to resort to an institutionalized solution, but it also has an inner circle with membership and functions that cannot be forced into the formal framework of an official cabinet committee. It is here, rather than in the cabinet itself, that crucial political compromises — for instance on the highly controversial co-determination program — have to be worked out between the coalition parties. But, of course, such informal, highest-level policy-making bodies can handle only a few political issues of major importance at any given time. They can, at times, resolve conflicts that otherwise might destroy the government coalition but they are surely unable to deal with the total volume of government policy that needs to be developed, evaluated, coordinated and approved day after day. This tremendous work load which constitutes the real substance of government policy cannot be handled by any presently existing central institution. The bulk of it is necessarily the product of intra-departmental and inter-departmental policy-making processes. Before these can be described and analyzed in much greater detail, at least a thumbnail sketch of the basic structure of the federal ministerial organization seems useful.

7. The ministerial organization

At present, the federal government consists of 16 ministries (of which two are managed by a single minister) which vary in size from the Ministry of Finance with a staff of about 1800 employees to the Ministry of Inner-German Relations with as few as 300 employees. Unlike American or British departments of the national government, the federal ministries in Germany do not usually have an administrative infra-structure of their own. Exceptions are the Ministry of Foreign Affairs with the foreign service, the Ministry of Defense with the armed services, the Ministry of

Transport with the federal railroad system, and the Ministry of Postal Services. In addition, there are a number of special purpose administrative agencies, finance corporations and research institutions directly attached to some of the federal ministries. They are limited, however, to performing nation-wide functions, while the administrative infra-structure for the regional and local implementation of federal policies is either provided by the states and by municipal governments or is entrusted to autonomous or semi-autonomous public corporations such as the social-insurance corporations or the unemployment-insurance and labor-market agency. As a consequence, most federal ministries should be regarded primarily as fairly large policy-making staffs rather than as administrative line organizations.

In order to understand the inter-departmental structure of the federal government, it is probably best to interpret it in terms of an incomplete matrix organization rather than in terms of a more conventional staff-line organization. While staff functions at the level of the Chancellor's Office and within the individual ministries have begun to develop, they must compete against a matrix structure that is solidly founded in the German organizational tradition and that operates at a government-wide level as well as within the ministries.

On the most general level, the ministerial organization has evolved out of the common continental pattern of the five 'classical' ministries of War, of Foreign Affairs, of Finance, of Justice and of Domestic Affairs. While the first four of these have by and large maintained their classical jurisdiction and functions, the Ministry of Domestic Affairs has been the fertile soil from which almost all other ministries have grown over the last century and a half. These new ministries, whose jurisdictions are frequently subdivided and reassembled in cabinet shuffles, can usually be defined in terms of a strong program orientation (like Research and Technology, Foreign Aid, or Housing and Urban Affairs) or in terms of a dominant clientele orientation (like Agriculture, or Labor) or a mixture of both (like Economic Affairs or Health, Youth and Family Affairs).

As this modern structure of special-purpose and special-interest ministries evolved, however, the classical ministries managed to retain generalist functions and to establish a grid-iron of functional authority across the evolving ministrial organization. This cross-cutting authority relationship is, of course, most obvious in the case of the Ministry of Finance which is responsible for drawing up

46

the annual budget and the financial plan of the government on the basis of bilateral negotiations with each of the other ministries. It must be consulted at an early stage by any ministry considering a policy proposal that might affect government revenue or expenditures. And under the rules and procedures of the government, in financial matters the minister of finance can be outvoted in the cabinet only with the concurrence of the chancellor. While under the law of the constitution all ministers appear to be equal, the minister of finance is definitely more equal than all the others.

In a similar (though less powerful) fashion the minister of justice has also retained his functional authority vis-à-vis the rest of the government. He is responsible for the constitutionality and legality of all government action and thus must be consulted in the drafting phase of all legislative proposals which need his clearance before they can be submitted for cabinet approval. Similarly, the minister of foreign affairs was responsible for maintaining all external contacts of the government regardless of the domestic distribution of jurisdictions among specialized ministries. The Foreign Office still retains much of this function, but with the increase of international and especially European regulation and the increasing need for substantive policy coordination across national boundaries, a number of other ministries have so intensified their international policy contacs that the Foreign Ministry has lost its former monopoly and now has to fight hard to achieve a minimum of foreign-policy coordination, especially in the areas of defense, foreign aid and agriculture. Finally, the Ministry of the Interior has retained its jurisdiction over the domestic civil service. It is responsible for developing and supervising civil service rules and regulations and it must be consulted in all cases of extraordinary appointments and promotions in the other departments. It also remains responsible for the development of the Joint Manual of Procedure of the federal ministries and it is consulted before basic changes in the organizational structure of other ministries are put into practice.

A fuller description of the present matrix structure would also have to include a number of examples where some of the newer ministries have gained or are claiming coordinating authority for the whole government in such fields as regional development, environmental protection, or civil defense. We shall return to these examples later. But at this more general level we may conclude with the observation that the traditional matrix structure of the German ministerial organization seems to perform a number of functions which in the United States, for instance, have been organized as central staff services in the Office of Management and Budget or in the Civil Service Commission. Given the relative effectiveness of its inter-ministerial matrix structure, the German government probably was less in need of developing strong central staff functions and, by the same token, it found it much more difficult to develop such central staff functions even in areas — such as government-wide planning — where the traditional matrix structure did not provide an adequate solution. The same ambiguity also exists at the level of intra-departmental organization, and we will take up both problems in later sections. Before we do so, however, we need to take a closer look at the training, the recruitment and career patterns, and the orientations of the people that operate the ministerial organization, the federal bureaucrats. It is they, working within the structural constraints of the ministerial bureaucracy and interacting with politicians of the departmental leadership, in the cabinet and in parliament, who necessarily must produce the substance of most federal policy. The political system's capacity for active policy-making is largely the capacity of its ministerial bureaucracy.

Chapter IV

THE FEDERAL BUREAUCRATS

The personal characteristics, the attitudes and orientation of an organization's members are obviously an important factor of organizational performance. We might therefore well have discussed the personnel of the federal departments as another resource of policy-making. This resource, however, is less specific to active policy-making in particular, and it is also less critical than the four prerequisites treated in chapter II, since the present "supply" of this resource lags less behind the demands of policy-making and since it also seems easier to improve shortcomings that do exist. It appeared moreover desirable to provide the reader with some background information about the actors in the federal bureaucracy before analyzing the departmental organization for policy-making in the following chapters. For these reasons we decided to devote a separate chapter to the ministerial personnel, which begins with a brief description of the civil service in the German Federal Republic and the place of federal bureaucrats within it. Our main interest, however, is in the attitudes and orientation of federal bureaucrats and in the factors shaping them.

1. The structure of the civil service

The federal bureaucracy is a rather small part of the whole public service. It accounts for less than 10 percent of the 3,2 mill. persons who are employed fulltime in public service [1]. Moreover, the federal bureaucracy's growth rate during the past two decades has been lower than that in other sectors of public administration; the highest growth rates were observed in the areas of health and education.

The public service in the Federal Republic employs three categories of personnel: civil servants, salaried employees, and wage-earning laborers. Civil servants (including judges) account today for only 45 percent of public employees. Salaried employees are historically speaking the youngest status group in the German public service. While the German state traditionally employed wage-earning laborers on a short-term contract basis in addition to tenured civil servants, salaried employees were taken on in significant numbers only after the turn of the last century. Since then the proportion of salaried employees and laborers in public service has increased continuously.

In legal theory, civil servants are distinguished from the other status groups by the functions they perform. The norms of constitutional law stipulate that tasks involving the exercise of public authority must be performed by civil servants. The rationale for these norms lies in the special loyalty to the state which is expected from civil servants, who are not permitted to strike and are subject to certain restrictions in their political activity. In fact, however, this functional basis of the status differentiation has long since eroded. In most sectors of the German public service employees work along-side civil servants performing identical functions. The three status groups are, however, characterized by a different distribution over the ranks. Laborers occupy mostly low-ranking positions, employees are found most frequently in the middle ranges, while civil servants are distributed over all ranks. This means that among the top ranks, the proportion of civil servants is well above the average 45 per cent.

Parallel to the attenuation of the functional distinction, the employment conditions of the different status groups have gradually become more similar. For instance, after 15 years of service the salaried employees achieve for all practical purposes the same degree of job security which the tenured civil servants enjoy. Similarly, while civil servants have a separate system of old age security, they do not — ceteris paribus — enjoy a noticeably higher income after retirement than the other two groups. More significant differences still exist in the recruitment, training, and career patterns of the different status groups. The Civil Service Reform Commission has recently recommended to abolish these largely disfunctional differences and to create one uniform status for all persons employed full-time in the public service. [2]

Along with the gradual disappearance of significant differences in the rights and duties associated with status, the attitudes of the status groups also seem to have become rather similar. In connection with the recent debate on civil service reform, several attitude studies were undertaken to show the extent to which tenured civil servants are still characterized by distinct attitudes. A study by Ellwein and Zoll showed that if age, sex, and educational background are held constant, differences between civil servants and public employees tend to disappear in all aspects of the syndrome of attitudes traditionally associated with civil service status, the so-called "Beamtenethos" already described by Max Weber in his picture of the ideal-typical official. [3] The same conclusion was reached in another large investigation inquiring into the attitudes and career patterns of over 2.000 members of the public service at all levels of the administrative pyramid. [4] Employees in public service and civil servants do have different views of their duties and obligations, of the nature of public service, of the proper relations with clients and with politics, and of the relative priority of private needs versus professional duties — but these differences are connected with differences in sex, rank, and type of work performed and are not caused by the differences in legal status.

The civil service in the Federal Republic is subdivided in the vertical dimension into four classes: the lower, medium, intermediate, and higher civil service. Horizontally each class is divided by function into a large number of categories, or "Laufbahnen", such as general administration, finance, teaching, health, and a large variety of technical specialties. The functional category "general administration" extends over all four classes, but this is not true of all functional categories. Each "Laufbahn", i.e. a functional category within a determinate class, is normally subdivided into five ranks, which constitute a career ladder. Training is specific for a given category, which virtually precludes horizontal mobility between functional categories. New recruits enter the civil service at the bottom rank of the category for which they qualify according to their training. Direct entry from outside into one of the higher ranking positions within a category is legally restricted, so that higher positions are usually filled by promotion from below.

Of the four classes, the medium and intermediate classes are the largest groups. The lower civil service is found mainly in the Federal Postal Service and the Federal Railroad; among civil servants in the federal and state administrations it accounts only for less than 5 percent. [5] The proportion of higher civil servants is largest in federal and state ministries, where all positions down to the section assistant, i.e. four to five levels down from the highest position, are reserved for higher civil servants.

A normal civil service career ends at the highest rank within the category entered at the beginning. Upward mobility into the next higher class is the exception rather than the rule and requires special ability, extensive further training, and the passing of an examination. Not quite 10% of civil servants have succeeded to move into a higher class than the one they originally entered.

The system just described, with its schematism of classes and categories, is easy to comprehend, facilitates the comparability of positions, and makes for the equality of individual promotion chances. It has obviously not been designed to increase efficiency by permitting personnel allocation to follow functional requirements. The boundary lines between classes and categories often do not correspond to any clear breaks in the difficulty of tasks or in the qualifications actually necessary to fulfill them. Potentially meaningful careers where the experience gained in performing a lower function serves as preparation for the next higher one often cut across the boundary between two classes. Conversely there are often no significant real differences in the job requirements of positions assigned to different ranks within a class, which means that the five-step pattern produces artificial differentiations. [6] These are serious handicaps for a flexible system of personnel management.

2. Recruitment and training

Recruitment and training are important factors in shaping the orientation and performance of federal bureaucrats engaged in policy-making. These are, as we have seen, in their majority higher civil servants. Civil servants in general are recruited for a career, that is for entry into a category and not, as other public servants, for specific positions. Their training accordingly is to enable them to fill a variety of positions. This "generalist" orientation holds especially for the functional category of general administration.

Most civil servants receive their occupational training wholly or in part by special training institutions within public administration. Within-service training is especially the rule for the medium and intermediate classes, and in general for the non-technical functional categories. Entry into the higher civil service requires academic training. Prospective higher civil servants enlist in the so-

52

called preparatory service, a combination of theoretical learning and on-the-job-training, and must pass a final examination in order to enter the civil service for good.

In the 19th century, the discipline of law had succeeded in Germany to supplant the evolving sciences of national economics and public administration in the teaching of future civil servants. [7] Since then, the functions of general administration in the higher civil service, still the most important category for the central national bureaucracy, have been reserved for jurists. Until about the first World War ministerial work was largely of a legal nature, so that law was in fact the preeminent educational requirement. But this has obviously changed with the diversification and extension of state functions and with the growing emphasis on planning.

Looking at the higher civil service as a whole, one can today no longer speak of a monopoly of jurists. This, however, is largely due to the increasing recruitment of non-legal professionals for service in the institutions of health and education and in a variety of technical functions, most of which are located at lower administrative levels. In the federal bureaucracy — and similarly in the state ministries — the diversification of the academic background of higher civil servants is less pronounced; here even today about 60% of higher civil servants have been trained in law — in spite of the fact that planning puts more emphasis on substantive expertise and that the ability to put a program into the appropriate legal form becomes a subordinate (though not unimportant) aspect of the task. Even more important, higher civil servants with a training in law have still a considerably better chance to reach top positions. [8] In the federal bureaucracy the leading positions down to the divisional level are still overwhelmingly occupied by jurists. This cannot but shape the perspective of federal bureaucrats.

It is, however, not only the formal training received which influences the orientation of higher civil servants. The structural and functional characteristics of the civil service as well as the special properties of civil service status result in a distinctive self-selective tendency among those university students who are attracted to the civil service. As a recent investigation has shown, the civil service attracts those students who, deviating from average student attitudes, emphasize the occupational values of job security, old age security, clearly structured tasks, and well circumscribed demands on one's abilities and time. [9] The more typical students who emphasize values such as autonomy in the work situation, an interesting job, and the chance to achieve more than average success in terms of income and position, are repelled rather than attracted by the perceived special characteristics of the civil service. In terms of personality characteristics it is similarly the atypical student with relatively high values in dogmatism, rigidity, and intolerance of ambiguity, who is attracted to the civil service. Interestingly enough this typical recruit is at the same time distinctly performance motivated. The higher civil service still seems to attract those who are by disposition a typically bureaucratic version of organization man.

This self-selective tendency appears dysfunctional from the viewpoint of personal characteristics favorable to the needs of active policy-making. The same is true within limits for the formal training of federal bureaucrats, which is, at least for the majority of them, quite deficient in many fields of knowledge which seem crucial for policy-makers. Nor does this apply to jurists only; the trained medical doctor or engineer also lack much of what they need for developing policy in their respective areas. The shortcomings of training and recruitment should not, however, be over-emphasized. Lacunae in formal training may be filled by experience and later learning, and the personality characteristics and value orientations which play a role in the self-selective tendency noted above may not be very directly related to specific qualities of policy. The effect of personal characteristics on organizational behavior can quite generally be modified and even superseded by the influence of structural features of the work situation.

3. The promotion system

Among the various features of the work situation the norms and procedures governing the career of civil servants play a specially important role in influencing organizational behavior. The criteria of promotion reflect the values of an organization. Through its selective and incentive functions, the promotion system brings these values to bear upon the behavior and orientation of civil servants.

The double-faced character of the federal bureaucracy which fulfills both implementative and policy-making functions inevitably produces tensions and contradictions in the system of norms and in the self-image of federal bureaucrats. This in turn is reflected in a certain ambivalence about the criteria of selection for top positions. A good instance of this is the diversity of attitudes towards partisan affiliation as a criterion of filling leading positions. Of all civil servants, federal bureaucrats and particularly the higher civil service are the group most favorably disposed toward the practice of taking party membership into account in filling leading positions down to the divisional level. [10] But even here the opinions are clearly divided and debates about the pros and contras of such a practice usually become very heated. In fact, there seem to exist side by side two conflicting sets of promotional criteria, one based on the traditional principles of the civil service and the other on more political considerations. Criteria belonging to the first set are: incorruptibility, loyalty, experience (seniority), professional competence, a good record of relations with peers and superiors. Criteria belonging to the second set are: partisan affiliation, political skills, the political support someone can muster or enjoys, and a record of good relations to one or more important client groups. The interpenetration of these two sets of criteria reflect a process of change in the federal bureaucracy's functional self-interpretation.

Officially, promotion is linked to capability and good performance, aside from a number of purely formal prerequisites which must be fulfilled. However, the criteria "capability" and "good performance" are not adequately operationalized, so that the existing system of periodic evaluations — to which moreover only civil servants are subjected — has a relatively low instrumental value. Only now are serious attempts being made to develop standardized objective instruments for the assessment of individual performance and capabilities. But the functional requirements of higher positions in public administration are in fact difficult to operationalize, maybe even more so than is true of managerial positions in industry; at least this may hold for positions requiring a high degree of political skills, as is the case in the federal ministries. This means that the superior's subjective interpretation of what constitutes "capability" will continue to be highly influential in promotional decisions, which in turn puts a premium on personal acquaintance and the familiarity growing out of long-term, stable work relationships. The realization that this is so is one of the factors which impede the horizontal mobility of federal bureaucrats.

It is difficult to establish empirically the relative weight of different selection criteria which are operative in filling the top positions in the federal ministries, especially as such criteria refer to performance qualities or to such personal characteristics as loyalty and incorruptibility. The recent study of career patterns already referred to was only able to refute the hypothesis of a generally negative selectivity, showing that respondents in leading positions contrasted positively with less successful colleagues in a number of personality characteristics. [11]

The promotion system does not only determine who gets into the higher positions where policy decisions are made. Promotion is also the most important performance incentive which the civil service disposes of, since the system of legally fixed remuneration for all status groups makes it impossible to use the financial incentive for stimulating individual performance, while other important rewards such as job security, old age pension, and social benefits are system rewards. [12] There is no doubt about the strong incentive character of promotion. While the attractiveness of the civil service is based to a large extent upon the system rewards and particularly the security which it offers, promotion is the means for achieving other important rewards: a higher salary, a more interesting job, the opportunity to exert influence and to achieve authority, prestige, and more individual autonomy. It is therefore not surprising that civil servants are characterized by high mobility aspirations. [13]

However, the desire to be promoted stimulates superior performance on the job only if promotion is perceived to depend on individual performance. This is not generally true, since promotion is to some extent a function of age and length of service. In the German civil service there exist two hierarchies side by side, without being strictly correlated: the hierarchy of formal ranks (upon which income depends), and the hierarchy of concrete positions. Advance in rank and promotion within the hierarchy of positions need not and often do not coincide. While this system may contribute to the satisfaction of those who have no more chances of achieving a higher position, it does obscure the meaning and hence the incentive effect of promotion.

Nevertheless, 69% of the respondents in the previously mentioned study of career patterns and career-related attitudes agreed that special efforts are needed to earn a promotion. [14] But there is no consensus about the performance equalities perceived as prerequisites of promotion. A large group in public service still considers qualities which belong to the syndrome of the civil servant's traditional ethos as favorable to promotion, while another group of similar size sees qualities such as professional competence, in-

56

itiative, and similar virtues of modern organization man as improving promotion chances.

In general, personal characteristics and individual behavior are not perceived as the most important preconditions of promotion. There is a wide-spread, explicit recognition of the importance of external factors which cannot be easily manipulated by the incumbent. Among these factors structural preconditions of promotion play a special role. Obviously a promotion requires first of all the incidence of a vacancy. Positions become available when the present incumbent is promoted or transferred. These are events which potential successors are rarely in a position to manipulate. But a position can also become available by newly creating it, and this event can more easily be influenced by an aspiring incumbent. The basic prerequisite for creating a new or upgrading an existing position is growth. Growth occurs when new programs are started or when already existing functions grow in importance and justify asking for more personnel. Individual efforts to create these favorable conditions for promotion may be an important motive force in the bureaucracy, but its aggregate effects can also be deleterious. Competition for new assignments or responsibilities, the extension of the hierarchy by introducing intermediate levels, the promotion of projects for other than objective reasons, and a general growth tendency, may all follow from individual efforts to influence the structural conditions of promotion.

The federal bureaucrat aspiring to be promoted is also in a difficult position because he is often judged by the success of his initiatives, which does not only depend on his own performance. Knowing that the failure of a personal initiative will react back upon his career while he runs no risk if he remains passive and demonstrates his commitment in other ways, the federal bureaucrat may be induced to shy away from developing policy initiatives with a high conflict potential and hence probability of failure. In this way the desire for career success may contribute to a reactive rather than active stance in policy-making.

4. The attitudes of federal bureaucrats

The relationship between the federal bureaucracy's functional character and the attitudes of its members is one of complex interdependence. What is expected of the federal bureaucracy in terms of an involvement in policy-making will affect the self-image and the attitudes of civil servants; but these attitudes in turn determine how the federal bureaucracy responds to the demands made on it. Should federal bureaucrats resist the expectation to become active in initiating policy and to engage in planning, and should they deny that this inevitably involves politics (though not necessarily partisan identification), the result would certainly be a low level of policy-making activity, no matter how urgent the external requests. On the other hand a widely prevailing "politicization" of federal civil servants can also have negative consequences, e.g. for the system of checks and balances between the legislative and executive institutions, for the continuity in policy-making, and even for the legitimacy of the political system. The self-perception and the attitudes of federal civil servants are therefore of considerable interest in the present context.

Until very recently the German civil servant has generally been perceived as the classical Weberian bureacucrat: legalistic in his orientation, a-political in his views, impartial in his judgment, an obedient instrument in the hands of his masters and a strict, impersonal superior to his subordinates. [15] Only recently empirical evidence has become available to show to what extent real changes have invalidated the classical image. Comparing the political attitudes of senior civil servants in several European countries, Robert D. Putnam found [16] — to his own obvious surprise — that his German respondents, all members of the federal bureaucracy, did not conform any more to the image of the "classical bureaucrat" than their British counterparts did, while Italian senior civil servants turned out actually to hold the attitides expected to characterize the German official.

Using data from intensive interviews and from questionnaire responses, Putnam distinguished two polar types, the "classical bureaucrat" and the "political bureaucrat". The classical bureaucrat believes that public issues can be resolved in terms of some objective standard of justice, he distrusts and rejects political institutions and is generally hostile to the world of politics. Political bureaucrats are favorably disposed towards the world of politics; the political bureaucrat is "...both more aware of 'political realities' and more willing to treat political influences on policy-making as legitimate. He recognizes the need to bargain and compromise, yet at the same time he does not shrink from advocating and even fighting for his own preferred policies". [17] As Putnam has shown, his two polar types are connected with a syndrome of related attitudes. Compared to classical bureaucrats, political buraucrats attach more importance to political ideals and programmatic objectives, they tend to reject the view that senior civil servants should limit their activities to the correct application of the law, they support political liberty, political equality, and popular participation more strongly, and they report more contacts with other participants in the policy process (such as politicians, interest group representatives, members of the government and of parliament), Putnam's German respondents were not only about as "political" in orientation, but also displayed these associated attitudes at least as much as their British colleagues did.

There was, however, a much greater diversity of orientation among German than among British respondents, a fact which again suggests a considerable extent of ambivalence in the self-perception and orientation of German federal bureaucrats. This attitudinal inhomogeneity, which also exists in other respects, is an important communication barrier in the federal bureaucracy.

Putnam discusses several possible explanantions for his unexpected findings. He points out that the "purges", i.e. the turnover in leading positions which occurred when the Social Democrats came to power in 1969, have played a minor role in shifting the orientation of the federal bureaucracy toward the "political" pole. Discounting the influence of a systematic bias produced by an interview situation in which German respondents attempt to display attitudes positively evaluated by their American interviewer, Putnam believes that the "essential clue" to the interpretation of his results lies in the age structure of the respondents.

The Italian senior civil servants are the oldest group and have served on the average much longer in public administration, with much less mobility between departments, than either German or British senior bureaucrats. The German respondents had the shortest average career in the national bureaucracy; more significantly still, they covered a much greater range of age and tenure than any of the other national samples. This clearly reflects the discontinuities and disruptions caused in the German civil service by the Nazi regime, World War II, and the emergence of the Federal Republic. According to Putnam, the orientation of German federal bureaucrats is strongly influenced by the political experience of a younger generation of officials which have come into leading positions more quickly due to the vacuum caused by the "missing generation", the age group decimated in World War II.

The predominant importance of age, or more correctly of generational membership, for the attitudes of German civil servants is corroborated by the previously quoted study of career patterns in public administration. This study included a number of attitudinal dimensions and showed that on the average German officials (including those of intermediate and medium rank) are characterized by the following attitudes: [18]

- a very pronounced clientele orientation: in developing a policy or implementing a program they feel bound to consider the interests of those who are affected by it — even if they are not prepared to subject public administration to the direct control of citizens;

- a rather pronounced legal orientation, even though the application of law is no longer perceived unanimously as the predominant function of public administration;

- a strong, but not emphatic or wholesale rejection of an identification with particular interest groups, and

- the view that whereas in practical matters such as working overtime the needs of the office may have priority over private inclinations, this does not hold where such priority would involve disavowing one's own political opinion.

Age differentiates strongly with respect to these attitudes. The younger officials are more willing to tolerate direct public control, they perceive their function less in terms of the application of law, they are more prepared to make themselves the spokesmen for group interests, and they are less prepared to subordinate their private interest and opinions to the demands of the office. Nor is this a function of age pure and simple, meaning that as they grow older, the younger officials will change their views and take on those of their elders. What is involved is rather a genuine generational difference [19]. This generational difference is connected partly with the political events of Germany's recent past, and partly with the changes in the position and function of public administration within society which have taken place and are still taking place.

These functional changes do not affect all groups within the civil service in the same way. While the activities of most civil servants, especially those working at lower administrative levels and in lower ranking positions, are still governed by legal norms which must be applied to individual cases and by programs which must be implemented, this is not typical for higher civil servants in the ministries. In view of what they actually do it is not surprising that higher civil servants — and especially those working in the federal bureaucracy — perceive the activity of the public official least of all groups in terms of the application and enforcement of legal norms. They are also more willing to subordinate their own private interests to the demands of the office, and reject the identification with interest groups most strongly. This is an interesting complement to Putnam's results: while the federal bureaucrat's awareness and acceptance of the political aspects of his job are growing, this need not automatically mean an increasingly partisan attitude, but may well go together with the felt obligation to consider all matters from the points of view of different groups.

Additional evidence about the orientation of federal bureaucrats was obtained by Grottian in a study on the attitudes of planners in the Bonn ministries [20]. Grottian interviewed 72 federal bureaucrats of various ranks, ranging from division head to section asistant, who were actively involved in the development of a number of specific programs. These federal "planners" were frequently recruited from outside of public administration. Fully a third had previously worked in a university or research institute — an unusually high proportion for the higher civil service in general.

Grottian concludes from his data that federal planners are not nearly as conservative, as "bureaucratic" in their orientation as is often believed. Most of them would probably have been classified as "political bureaucrats" by Putnam. As many federal planners give priority to socio-political policy goals (such as equality of opportunity, democratization, social justice, and income redistribution) as give precedence to system stability and economic goals; most frequently federal planners support a combination of these two types of policy goals.

On the whole this means that there is adequate attitudinal support for the SPD's "policy of internal reforms" among higher civil servants actually involved in policy-making. It is interesting, however, that while Grottian's respondents perceive the Federal Republic's socio-political system mostly in terms of a pluralistic model, every second one of them attributes the failure to realize important policy goals to the lack of popular understanding rather than to the restrictions inherent in the capitalist economy or the way the political institutions function. This may be considered an indicator of political naivete — or of a hidden elitism among federal planners.

Aggregating his results to a typology of planners, Grottian finds that fully 50% of his sample can be classified as "actively oriented towards structural change" or at least "oriented towards structural modifications". The first of these sub-groups is characterized by a specially high incidence of party membership and of professional experience in science institutions (universities and research institutes). Both groups oriented toward the reform rather than the conservation of existing structures have a significantly lower average age. This confirms once more the earlier evidence of a strong generational difference in the political attitudes of federal bureaucrats.

Taking the evidence of these various studies together it can be said that federal bureaucrats involved in policy-making are by and large characterized by attitudes favorable to the fulfillment of their function. However, this is so not because of, but rather in spite of the current civil service system with its typical patterns of training, recruitment, and promotion.

Chapter V

DEPARTMENTAL ORGANIZATION

1. The formal structure of the federal bureaucracy

After the presentation of the personnel system of the federal bureaucracy we will now continue our discussion of the organizational structure at the level of individual ministries. As will be recalled, there are at present 16 of them, ranging in size from just over 300 to about 1800 employees. If these numbers seem small in international comparison, it should also be remembered that most ministries at the federal level have no administrative infra-structure of their own and do not have the right of detailed supervision over the administrative implementation of federal statutes through state and local governments. Their main function is policy development and policy revision with federal legislation and federal spending programs as the major policy instruments at their disposal. Within the departments, policy-making activities account for roughly one half of the total work load, with considerable variations between individual units. The other half is divided between program implementation àt the national level, the supervision of administrative agencies attached to federal ministries, staff and information functions performed for the departmental executive, the cabinet and parliament and, of course, internal management and housekeeping functions.

In their formal authority structure, federal ministries still correspond to the monocratic model associated with the normative theory of ministerial responsibility. All actions of the ministry are legally attributed to the minister himself who, alone, is held to be politically responsible to parliament (even though parliament cannot formally hold individual ministers accountable through a vote of non-confidence). Regardless of the routine allocation of functions within the ministry, the minister may reserve for himself any decision including, of course, personnel decisions and organizational decisions. As a matter of fact, ministers do usually reserve to themselves all personnel decisions within the higher civil service and all promotions.

The further organization of the ministries follows monocratic principes as well. Below the top leadership level of the minister and the state secretaries, departments are organized into divisions which in turn are subdivided into sections. When the number of sections in a division increases beyond 7 or 8, the division is often split into two or more subdivisions, each headed by its own subdivisional chief. The sections as the basic working units of the ministerial organization vary considerably in size but, as we shall see below, most of them are quite small. There are altogether about 1600 sections in the federal government. Even though the departmental structure seems to correspond fully to the principles of monocratic, hierarchical organization, it should be noted that its working capacity is almost entirely concentrated at the lowest hierarchical level. As will be shown below, hierarchical authority relations are not supported by an organizational structure that would provide the hierarchy with substantial staff services. If ministries really were governed from the top down, one would expect much more manpower available at the higher ranks. At this point, one might remember the relative weakness of central staff functions at the cabinet level, which have remained under-developed because many of the decision-making functions transcending individual ministries are effectively taken care of by a matrix structure which assigns cross-sectional responsibilities to the Ministries of Finance, Foreign Affairs, Justice and the Interior. With certain variations, this basic pattern of a matrix organization is repeated at the departmental level. Here, the jurisdiction of most divisions is also defined in terms of their program responsibilities or in terms of specific clienteles, that is with a view to their policy outputs. But in each ministry, there is also a 'division Z' (Z for "Zentral") in which cross-cutting management and service functions for the whole department are centralized. In addition to the technical and housekeeping services, these will always include budgetary, personnel, and organization functions. In many departments, the central division also provides legal services and, in some, research coordinating services. In others, a separate division combining statistical services and computerized information systems with department-wide program-planning functions has been established. And in two ministries, Foreign Affairs and Foreign Aid, the matrix structure extends into a third dimension, adding divisions organized by area to the output and the service divisions. In other ministries, such as Transport or Economic Affairs, an area structure is used to define the responsibilities of sections within some output divisions.

At the divisional level, a matrix organization is less universal but still quite frequent. Thus, specialized divisions which are largely staffed by physicians, natural scientists, or engineers, usually maintain a legal section which is responsible for translating the substantive contributions of specialist sections into workmanlike draft legislation. Elsewhere, a research section may maintain the contacts to the scientific community and manage research contracts for the rest of the division. Many larger divisions also have 'general policy sections' for the purpose of developing a coherent framework for the more specialized policy activities of the division. However, such general policy sections will often be frustrated in their intended functions and may end up as 'waste basket units' responsible for residual chores unclaimed by other sections.

The effectiveness of this two and even three-level matrix structure of the federal government is strongly reinforced by well developed channels of lateral communication by-passing the formal hierarchy. Thus, the budget sections within the Z-division of any ministry will operate in very close contact with the budget division of the Finance Ministry and they are, in terms of their skills and perspectives, as much the bridgehead of Finance within their own department as they are the spokesmen for departmental interests in their dealings with the budget division. Similarly, the legal sections will have more intensive contacts with the Ministry of Justice, and the heads of the organization sections of all ministries are all members of an interministerial working group under the chairmanship of the organization division in the Ministry of the Interior.

From the point of view of output-oriented divisions, the centralization of personnel management in division Z appears particularly irritating. They do recognize the need for central allocation and reallocation of available positions among competing departments. But when the choice among candidates for recruitment to available positions and for promotion within a division is also monopolized by the central personnel unit, there is often a clash of interests. On the one side, section chiefs and division heads are under pressure to recruit the most qualified candidates for their specific functions. They also see promotions within the division as an important incentive and as a reward for performance which they are best able to observe and feel best qualified to judge. On the other hand, the central personnel section is legitimately concerend with the flexibility of the personnel system as a whole which may be impaired by the recruitment of specialists who could not be employed in other divisions of the department, and it must be very much concerned with the equity of promotion decisions which, if unduly favourable, will immediately become precedents for many other claimants. Thus, the need for 'orderly' personnel management will often conflict with the personnel needs of output-oriented divisions with the consequence of a permanent tug-of-war between division chiefs and the personnel section. In practice, both are often overridden by political considerations of the departmental leadership which may see a need to use personnel decisions for strategic purposes especially at the higher levels of the civil service. As a consequence, personnel decisions and civil service careers above the level of section head become highly unpredictable and are so perceived by civil servants themselves. [1]

But personnel decisions are atypical in the degree of leadership attention which they receive. In other areas, the matrix functions of division Z cannot be similarly interpreted as a kind of preparatory staff work supporting leadership decisions. By and large, the matrix units are on their own, interacting with the rest of the department in horizontal communication, bargaining and decision processes, relying on their formal veto powers, their substantive expertise, and the close contacts with their respective matrix ministries rather than upon the departmental leadership. To put the matter very pointedly: the ministries of the German federal government have not developed more substantial staff services at the leadership level because their matrix structure permits them to function with a minimum of leadership involvement in all routine operations. As will become clear in later sections, however, neither the bureaucratic routine of division Z nor the intermittent and haphazard interventions of an overworked and understaffed leadership are able to provide optimal conditions for the increasing tasks of active policy development within the ministerial bureacracy.

66

2. The basic operating units

A major feature of the policy-making process in the federal departments is its considerable decentralization. It is obvious that the
sections, the basic operating units of departmental organization,
work out the proposals for new programs in detail. There is little
institutionalized capacity for this work elsewhere in a department,
and neither the departmental executive nor the divisional leadership are able to participate very actively in the drafting of proposals. In addition, however, the sections also play an important role
in initiating policy proposals. In fact it can be said that most
policy proposals in the federal departments are initiated by the
sections, if by initiating we mean not simply to utter an idea but
to decide that a more or less clearly conceptualized policy goal
shall be transformed into a proposal for a new program or program
change, and to sit down oneself to start work on it or direct
somebody else to do so.

Of course, policy-making is continuous, and it is difficult to
establish where one policy-making process ends and another begins. In tracing the genesis of a specific policy output it is therefore often difficult to identify any one person or group as
initiator. Policy initiatives are often the product of a process of
discussion going on between different units and different hierarchical levels where even the participants cannot reconstruct with
certainty at which point this discussion process crystallized into an
initiative and who was responsible for it. But even taking this
relative uncertainty into consideration, it can safely be said that
policy initiatives in the sense here defined originate in the majority
of cases in the sections rather than at higher levels or in
parliament. This may contradict the self-image of some ministers
and senior officials, but it conforms to the rules which authorize
the sections to initiate policy, and is supported by widely shared
informal expectations.

By virtue of the role which the sections play in the process of
policy-making, their structural features and mode of operation
may influence the quality of policy output importantly. It is with
a view to this question that we now turn to an analysis of the
major structural and operational features of the sections.

2.1 Size and structure of sections

The first striking characteristic is the small size of most sections.

Disregarding for the moment the sections in division Z and those which serve staff functions for the departmental executive, we find that two thirds of the sections count 1 to 6 members; most frequent are sections with 3, 4 and 5 members [2].

The sections are composed of four types of members: *Referent* (section head), *Hilfsreferenten* (section assistants), *Sachbearbeiter*, and clerical personnel. Smaller sections often do not dispose of a full-time secretary and hence contain no clerical personnel. In some departments the pool system is used to organize clerical assistance, though this is not the solution preferred by most section members. A typical section of four members may thus consist of the section head, one section assistent, and two *Sachbearbeiter*. The number of *Sachbearbeiter* in a section is on the average slightly higher than that of assistants.

Section head and section assistants belong to the higher civil service, the latter being normally one or two (maximally three ranks below the section head. In contrast, *Sachbearbeiter* belong to the intermediate class of the civil service which means that they have no academic training and normally do not expect to move up to the position of section assistant. *Sachbearbeiter* are formally responsible for doing routine tasks and assisting the section head and section assistants in their more demanding activities, but due to their often long experience with the work in a given section they may develop a high level of expertise, so that the qualitative difference between their activities and those of a section assistant is sometimes quite small.

In spite of their different educational level and their belonging to different classes of the civil service, section assistants are not formally superior to the *Sachbearbeiter*. Both report directly to the section head, so that sections have formally only two hierarchical levels (disregarding clerical personnel). This situation is resented by many section assistants, and in fact an informal hierarchy of three levels often develops.

The small size of the sections is a traditional feature of ministerial organization. That this has not changed as the departments became bigger is due to several reasons. Prominent among them are the constraints of personnel policy, which produce a tendency to increase the number rather than the size of sections. To keep the hierarchies of rank and of position related to each other, it is for instance common practice not to promote somebody in the position of section assistant beyond a certain rank, so that further promotion depends on the chance of moving into the position of section head. The opportunities for rewarding deserving officials thus depend importantly on the number of sections which exist. The existence of many small sections also increases the chances to recruit needed specialists from outside who could not be had for less than salary of a section head.

Another reason for the smallness of the sections is the persisting prevalence of the hierarchical principle. The section head is fully responsible for all activities of his section. This principle of one-man responsibility again makes for an increase in the number rather than in the size of sections. The section head's general accountability makes it risky for him to delegate important matters to his subordinates. If he is to be held fully accountable for the unit's activities, these must therefore remain sufficiently restricted in scope and number to permit him control over them. To split a section into two small ones is hence preferred to letting it grow too much.

The principle of one-man responsibility also constitutes an important barrier for the development of a more team-like structure within the sections. The section head's general accountability pushes him to play the role of hierarchical superior whether he wants it or not. Though a certain amount of delegation at least to the section assistants has been introduced officially, this usually concerns only matters of smaller importance, or routine tasks. Normally section assistants receive clearly defined assignments from the section head and enjoy little independence, which is the major grievance of this group of federal bureaucrats.

Since sections are relatively small, the section head does not limit himself to fulfill leadership and management functions. He normally participates fully in the substantive work, where he tends to be less narrowly specialized than his subordinates because he cannot limit his attention to some part only of the section's activities. Assignments of special importance, primarily those of a politically delicate nature, the section head usually performs himself. He also represents the section in its contacts with the environment, both within and outside of the bureaucracy. Section assistants sometimes complain about this "monopolization" of all important contacts by the section head.

An important structural feature of departmental organization which is not directly related to the question of section size is the existence of a very detailed, even fragmented division of labor. In every department there exists an official task allocation plan which allocates in an enumerative way specific tasks to the individual sections, and even to individual members within sections. As far as possible, task allocation within a department is thus fixed rather than ad hoc, and it is elaborately specified. Where the official task allocation plan of a department is not detailed down to the level of individual members, a rather fixed distribution of tasks within sections evolves nevertheless.

Of course there are limits to the fixed allocation of assignments. These limits are connected with the specific nature of ministerial work: the unique, the unforeseeable, and new tasks can obviously not be permanently allocated. Changes even in the more lasting activities of a department are frequent, and pervasive enough to make revisions of the official task allocation plan necessary at rather short intervals. The responsibility to update the task allocation plan lies with the unit in division Z which is concerned with organizational matters.

The existence of an official task allocation plan has definite advantages. It facilitates finding out who is the responsible person for any given matter. It makes the distribution of assignments a routine matter for division chiefs and section heads. The fixed task allocation is also a personal safe-guard in so far as it delimits precisely what anybody can be asked to do and what he need not do. For the same reason the principle of fixed task allocation reduces conflict over responsibilities, both where several units compete for an attractive assignment or where they want to avoid being burdened with an unattractive one. These advantages explain the resistance which all attempts to weaken or abolish the principleof fixed and detailed task allocation have met so far. However, this principle is more appropriate for administrative agencies which implement programs. Where instead new programs are to be developed, the fixed and detailed allocation of tasks constitutes an element of rigidity and impedes the flexible adjustment of the organization to new demands and to changes in its activities.

The small size and the principle of fixed task allocation combine to produce a tendency for each section to work very intensively within a very limited substantive area. The attention of each section is focused on — and rather strictly limited to — a small sector of the environment. This fragmentation of responsibilities at the section level has the advantage of producing a high degree of problem sensitivity, of expertise, and of competence to deal with the problems arising in a small specified area. The disadvantages of this structural feature become visible only against the background of the previously discussed prerequisites for an active policy.

2.2 Policy development at the section level

Policy-making can be described as the selective transformation of policy inputs into outputs. Selective criteria operate at several stages of this process. The criteria may be different ones at each stage. A first weeding-out occurs where from the steady flow of incoming impulses — ideas, criticisms, demands — a few are picked up by the policy-making system and are made the object of a policy initiative.

The impulses for initiatives originating in the section come from the observation of developments in the field, from contact with the clientèle, or from the feed-back produced by presently operating programs. This last source of impulses is of particular importance for the sections, who learn from the implementing agencies of flaws in current programs. Organized interests, on the other hand, also turn to higher levels or political groups to press their claims. By virtue of their organizational location, the sections enjoy in fact a relative insulation against external pressure, so that that the inclination of powerful organizations to instrumentalize the sections and transform them into loyal advocates of their interests is smaller than one might believe. Sections are also able to choose the role of advocate for relatively weak interests. This for instance is true of several sections in the Department of Health which deal with consumer protection, and food and drug control.

The relative autonomy of the sections in policy-making depends partly upon the point in time at which higher levels are consulted and thus have the chance to stop the initiative then and there or to have it modified according to their own views. Actual practice varies considerably in this respect. As far as the sections themselves are concerned, they tend to discuss an initiative with superiors the earlier the more important they consider it to be. However, the section is often not free to decide when to present a proposal to its superiors; this also depends on the directives of the departmental leadership, which follow no uniform pattern. In general, the immediate superior will be informed in an informal way rather early in the process. The divisional leadership must then decide at what stage to inform the departmental executive, unless there are specific directives to be followed. In one department, for instance, we learned of a general directive that all program initiatives had to be presented in the form of a brief statement to the departmental executive and could only be worked out in detail when endorsed by the executive. But in most departments the executive comes to know a program initiative stemming from the section level only when a detailed written proposal is passed up to it through channels.

The number of policy impulses received at the section level is generally much larger than could possibly be taken up and transformed into policy initiatives. Impulses must therefore possess a certain urgency before they will be acted upon. This has been described by Sharkansky as "waiting until problems impose themselves". [3] But it is not simply the urgent impulse or the demand which presents itself loudly enough which triggers a policy initiative. There are other criteria of selectivity operating at the section level which are determined by the characteristic structural properties of the section organization, in particular its small size and low power, which influence which impulses will be taken up and acted upon. The operation of these selective criteria is reinforced by certain characteristic attitudes of the higher civil servants staffing the ministries. The most important selective criteria can be grouped under two headings: they are either criteria of manageability or criteria determining the probable success of an initiative.

The smallness of the sections and the restricted scope and clearly bounded nature of their areas of responsibility focus attention upon a small segment of the environment and operate against the perception of large problems which cut across the system of fragmented responsibilities, something which is characteristic especially of problems calling for an active policy. More precisely, such problems may be seen, but the individual section shies away from tackling them on its own initiative because in doing so it would either run the risk of getting involved in conflicts over formal responsibility with other sections, or it would have to embark upon the tortuous road of getting these other sections to cooperate in a joint venture. The chance of easily finding such cooperation is reduced by the restricted work capacity of small sections. Every section's time budget is largely used up by completing projects already under way and by work in response to authoritative requests and directives from superiors, not to mention the time which many sections must spend on implementing programs. Lack of time makes a section reluctant to respond favorably to requests for cooperation, and this in turn can dissuade the initiating section from asking for such cooperation, especially since the risk of failure also grows with the need for support and cooperation. The result is a general tendency for sections to restrict their initiatives to problems falling into their own area of responsibility, i.e. to problems of smaller scope. The situation is different only where the benefits of a cooperative venture would accrue primarily to the initiating section rather than being dispersed among many units, so that the expectation of visible success may outweigh the costs and risks of getting a joint venture started.

The extent to which it is possible for a section to find problems which it can approach without needing the cooperation of other units depends not only on the scope of its area of responsibility, but also on the functional division of labor in a department. Where for instance the legal and the non-legal experts for a given subject matter belong to different sections, it is not possible at all for one section to start a new project without involving another one. By increasing the need for cooperation the matrix type of organization can thus impede decentral policy initiatives.

The inclination to prefer problems which a section can handle without depending too much on the help and cooperation of other units is connected with another important tendency, i.e. the tendency to externalize the costs of a new project. The realization of most policy goals has repercussions in other policy areas, and some of these side-effects will be negative in terms of other policy goals. The attempt to foresee such side-effects of one's own project and maybe even to point them out to the affected sections would make the job more difficult for the initiating section by provoking resistance and increasing the need for negotiation, which means to increase the section's dependence on other groups. To proceed in this way might be good for the quality of policy output, but it goes against the interest of the initiating section. The result is a tendency to neglect especially the remoter side-effects of a new project and to wait for those who are detrimentally affected to speak up for themselves — which they often can do only when it is too late to take account of their interests in the formative stage of a new policy.

The limited working capacity of the small section militates also against tackling a problem in a section's own area of responsibility if this requires too much time for collecting information, drafting etc. It also discourages the sections to take up problems which are well recognized, but "too big" in terms of the time necessary to develop a proposal — unless directed to do so by superiors. It is characteristic that in cases where the executive finally decided that a problem which appeared of unmanageable size to the responsible section must nevertheless be taken up, the section's working capacity also had to be temporarily enlarged, not seldom by the creation of a commission or by the temporary delegation of additional staff "on leave" from other administrative units. One characteristic example for this was the establishment of the Civil Service Reform Commisssion. A particular subdivision in the Ministry of the Interior was formally responsible for all changes to be made in civil service law, but its work capacity was largely taken up by pressing day-to-day tasks and its power was too small to tackle the job of a comprehensive civil service reform which unavoidably interferes with some powerful interests. The formally responsible unit in the bureaucracy accepted and in a way even welcomed the establishment of a special commision, admitting that it could not have developed a comprehensive reform proposal within the same period of time. The commission was not only able to get scientists and representatives of the major interest to work together, it also disposed of a large (temporary) staff and of considerable sums of money for research and consultation fees. Other examples of similar import are provided by the commission for the reform of food and drug legislation, the commission for the development of a program of environmental protection, or the commission for territorial reorganization.

Problems of manageable size often derive from existing legislation or programs in the course of implementation, if their solution calls for little more than an amendment or a program modification: incremental changes, in short. This is the type of problem a section will most easily pick up and transform into a policy initiative. Policy-making therefore means overwhelmingly to improve on existing policy rather than starting something entirely new.

Problems may be manageable for a section, but other reasons may still speak against their being chosen as subject matter for a policy initiative. There is a tendency to avoid initiatives which are certain to meet with vociferous resistance by important social groups, as well as initiatives which are politically not feasible and would be sure not to find support in the cabinet and/or parliamant. Similarly there is a tendency to avoid initiatives which would lead to conflict with more powerful units in the same or in other departments. There is also little spontaneous desire to develop initiatives generally held to be utopian or initiativves which would be extremely costly. In every case what is involved is a judgment as to what could impede the success of a policy initiative, success meaning that it "goes through", i.e. is accepted by the higher levels and in the end, if necessary, by the cabinet and/or parliament. As we pointed out before, it is important for a civil servant's career to become identified with successful projects and even more, not to become identified with a failure. The effect of this motivational factor is reinforced by a structural one, since the greater visibility of the individual in a small work unit makes it easier to attribute initiatives to individual persons and hence makes them all the more wary of risky ventures.

The tendency to avoid initiatives of a politically delicate nature is strongly suppported by a second attitudinal factor, the self-image of the higher civil servant as non-partisan. While a higher civil servant in a federal department will be politically oriented in the sense of taking "political realities" into consideration and also in the sense of playing the power game in order to see his project through, he will shy away from becoming identified with a particular political party. Therefore he may avoid developing initiatives in a matter where this can only mean taking sides in a partisan issue. Matters which are politically delicate in this and related senses are defined as the proper field for executive initiative. This reluctance to become involved in conflicts which are strictly of a partisan nature is strongest at the section level, where the non-partisan expert is still the model image. Section heads are normally career civil servants, while — as we shall see below — division heads come increasingly to be political appointees, in the sense of having been chosen for the position on the grounds of political reliability in a distinctly partisan perspective, and are therefore less reluctant to become involved in matters which bear a partisan character.

The probability of success as selection criterion finally contributes toward a distinct time patterning of policy initiatives at the section level. In the beginning of a legislative period, especially if this is accompanied by a change in the governing majority and/or a change in the positions of department head, there is a tendency for many initiatives to originate at the section level, largely because at this time the chances for realization are especially good with four years still ahead to pursue the matter and with a certain openness as to the new government's policy intentions. At the same time a new department head often welcomes section initiatives at the beginning of his term of office, as these are an important source of information for him about what is going on in the department. Towards the middle of the legislative period section initiatives can count on getting less executive attention, or getting it with more difficulty. At this time the department's work schedule for the rest of the legislative period is more or less fixed and the chances for putting yet another program on the agenda become increasingly worse. Towards the end of the legislative term, it needs high urgency (defined in political terms) for any new matter to be taken up by a department, and in this case it is more likely the departmental executive who initiates action than a section. The influence of the rhythm of legislative periods is of course mitigated if the coming election will in all probability not lead to a change in the ruling majority.

In the preceding discussion we have focused our attention on the policy-initiating function of the sections. This selective perspective should not create the mistaken impression that the sections operate quite autonomously in this field, restricted only by the needs of horizontal cooperation and the anticipated resistance of higher levels and political organs. It should be remembered that policy-making is only one among several functions of the federal bureaucracy, and developing policy initiatives takes up only the smaller part of time which the sections devote to policy-making. Most of it goes to the drafting, discussing, revising, and refining of proposals, i.e. to work in the post-initiation phases. Nor are the sections free from direction and control in developing programs. The sections are in fact not even free to structure their own work schedule, but must give priority to what is important and urgent in the view of the departmental leadership — unless they happen to work outside of the leadership's sphere of attention. This will become clear in the discussion of divisional leadership and especially oof executive control.

2.3 Alternative types of basic operating units

The disadvantages of the current mode of sectional organization especially for program development have not gone unnoticed, and attempts have been made to introduce alternative types of basic units. One of these, the so-called project groups (or task forces), is based on the team principle. Team organization is of superior efficiency only under rather special conditions which obtain where within a limited period of time a very complex problem requiring a large variety of different kinds of expertise must be solved. [4] Project groups are accordingly established ad hoc for a limited period of time and for a specified planning task. Their members are drawn from the permanent operating units, to which they continue to belong, being relieved of part or all of their normal

76

functions for the duration of their membership in the project group.

Project groups exist today both within and between departments. They are typically established where problems must be solved which cut across the defined areas of responsibility of several sections, divisions, or even departments. But the recognized need for cooperative problem solving is only one motive for the establishment of project groups. Sometimes a project group serves the main purpose of temporarily enlarging the work capacity of a small permanent unit, and at times the high valuation of team work as such has motivated the institution of a project group.

Within a project there exist no hierarchical levels; the group forms a team, with the leader as primus inter pares. This is expressed in the style of work and in the fact that members of different rank work together as equals. Most members of project groups occupy positions as section assistant; division and sub-division chiefs are rarely found as members in a project group. Many project groups exist for less than a year, though there are also cases where a project group becomes a semi-permanent institution.

A major feature of project groups is their relative autonomy. Often their members are explicitly not bound by specific directives from their regular superiors as far as their work in the project group is concerned. This makes for more flexibility and less conflict in the process of joint problem solving. Accordingly the main importance of project groups lies in the area of horizontal coordination; this function will be discussed more in detail in chapter VIII.

While project groups have become an ubiquitous phenomenon in all federal departments, sometimes even to the extent of constituting a serious drain on the work capacity of the sections, another new type of basic unit is still being experimented with. This is a new type of permanent unit, considerably larger than the normal section it is designed to supplant, and characterized by a so-called "group structure". Group structure does not mean team structure, however. The group has a leader who is of a higher rank than the normal section head; he concentrates on fulfilling leadership and management functions for the group. A group typically includes several members of the personal rank corresponding to the position of section head. In one of the group models experimented with, the hierarchical distinction between "Referent" and "Hilfsreferent" has also been relinquished, along with the traditional position titles which were uniformly changed into "group member". Recently the Ministry of the Interior has started to sponsor a program of experimentation in the course of which several departments will introduce group-structured divisions for a trial period. Earlier the Department of Housing and Urban Affairs had reorganized one of its divisions according to the "group structure" principle. But the experience in this case has been somewhat discouraging. It was hoped that the greater number of highly qualified members in the group would make for a more cooperative style of work, and hence for more flexibility in the internal distribution of tasks, enabling the unit to cope better with variations in the volume and mix of work demands. In fact, however, the former hierarchical relations and the old pattern of fixed task distribution reasserted itself under the cover of the new formal organization. At least in the first period after their establishment the groups in the Ministry of Housing and Urban Affairs did not function very differently from the way in which the previously existing subdivisions had operated.

3. Divisional leadership

The division head and, where subdivisions exist, the subdivision heads constitute the divisional leadership. Since subdivisions are a consequence of gradual organizational growth, there are still many divisions which are not subdivided. The subdivision head introduces an additional level into the departmental hierarchy. Section heads in a subdivided division are hierarchically even further removed from the department top, and division heads loose at least some of the direct contact with the details of work in the sections. Both division chiefs and section heads see therefore certain disfunctions connected with the introduction of subdivisions, notwithstanding the recognized necessity for doing so where the number of sections in a division becomes too large.

The divisional leadership has no associated staff units. The division head has normally a full-time secretary (which is not true of all sub-division heads), but officially no other help. Occasionally a member from one of the division's sections may informally serve as part-time assistant to the division chief. While this points to an unfulfilled need, the divisional leadership itself does not press to obtain a fulltime staff. The restricted working capacity of the divisional leadership does however influence the functions that can be fulfilled at this level.

78

3.1 Functions of divisional leaders

The functions of the divisional leadership derive in part from its position within the departmental organization. Located at the interface between the operating units and the top executive, the divisional leaders must first of all mediate between these levels. This means on the one hand to direct the work of the division according to the general directives of the departmental executive, to transmit specific requests from the departmental leadership to the sections and to see that they are fulfilled. It means on the other hand to represent the views of the division to the departmental executive and to promote its projects in dealings with other parts of the system. Divisional leaders differ in the emphasis they put on the downward or the upward direction of this mediating function, but extreme cases of identification either with the sections versus the top executive or vice versa are rare. In general the function of mediating between the levels is accepted as characteristic of divisional leadership by all incumbents.

A second major function of divisional leaders is to represent the division in relations with the environment and to coordinate its activities with those of other divisions and other departments. These external relations are often fraught with conflict and involve bargaining and other strategies of defending the interests of the division or the department in a given issue. Since these contacts are of crucial importance for the work of the division, it is not surprising that most divisional leaders see a major function here.

Managerial tasks form the third major group of divisional leadership functions. This includes functions related to budgeting, personnel management, and organization, but also planning and coordinating the work of the sections. For the first set of functions there exist specialized units within division Z. This restricts the authority of divisional leaders in makig personnel, budget, and organizational decisions for their division, but since they participate in the corresponding decision processes, these administrative tasks are very time-consuming nevertheless.

Of the other managerial functions, coordination is more prominent than planning. There is little systematic planning of future activities at the divisional level. The division must respond continuously to unforeseen demands coming from the top leadership as well as from the environment, so that detailed long-range or even medium-range planning of division activities is hardly feasible. What can be done and usually is being done is a rough time-scheduling of individual projects. Occasionally the time schedules for several projects are aggregated for the division or, if the minister requires it, even for the whole department. But this serves primarily a documentation (and, if carried to higher levels, an information) function and hardly amounts to substantive planning. Coordination, on the other hand, is a standard task of divisional leaders, though the extent to which they are engaged in coordinating activities varies with the type of work performed in the division and the degree of interdependence between its sections. In some divisions, the sections work rather independently of each other in neighboring, but not interrelated areas. Where there is more interdependence between sections and where policy proposals are worked out jointly by several sections of a division, the divisional leadership can be more involved in coordination.

3.2 Role choices of divisional leaders

Depending on the relative emphasis they put on their different functions and depending particularly on the dominating identification either with the top executive or with the basic operating units, divisional leaders can define their role in rather different ways. The basic role choice for divisional heads is between the "bureaucrat", or traditional civil servant, and the "politician". The "bureaucrat" is a career civil servant who reached this leadership position by moving up stepwise in the departmental hierarchy. He avoids identification with a political party and with party politics, and his personal authority is based on expertise rather than on political group membership. This type of division head still recognizes his mediating function, but in the case of conflict he sides with the sections rather than with the political executive.

The development of the "politician" is greatly furthered by the institution of so-called political civil servants, a *contradictio in adjecto* according to the traditional understanding of the civil service which is, however, in accord with the needs of policy-making under present conditions. [5] The definition of "political civil servant" applies to the ranks of state secretary and to the one directly below, the "Ministerialdirektor", which is the rank to which most division heads belong. These two ranks can be temporarily retired at the discretion of the government (cabinet and ultimately the president) without any need for disciplinary action — the only way in which a civil servant can normally be removed from active service or relieved of his post. This legal provision in and by itself may do no more than exert a certain pressure on division heads to prove themselves "politically reliable" or to be at least sufficiently responsive to the political intentions of the majority party or ruling coalition, and to the minister's party in particular. But there has also been a change in the recruitment practice of division heads. While moving up within the departmental hierarchy has traditionally been the normal route of access to these positions, recruitment of division heads from outside of the federal bureaucracy is today becoming more frequent. Such external recruits will normally become civil servants, though they may enter the service as employees. But they are usually members or at least outspoken partisans of (one of) the ruling party(ies). Such an official's career is bound up with the fate of the government, he identifies with its political program and expects to be relieved of his post in case of a change of government. This makes him accept the political content of his role, and often he states quite explicitly that his major orientation as division head is a political one. In general his subordinates perceive him in the same way, as a partisan political promoter and representative of the departmental executive rather than as speaker of the sections.

Though "bureaucrat" and "politician" are the major role alternatives at the divisional level, it is possible to distinguish further three variants of the bureaucrat role which may be called the "professional expert", the "non-partisan promoter", and the "administrator". The professional expert role is based on substantive expertise and is characterized by the regular and active participation in the work of the operating units and especially in the details of program development. The non-partisan promotor likewise possesses professional competence, but emphasizes the tasks of building up support and resolving conflicts in order to promote the projects developed in his division, pushing them through to final approval. The "administrator" finally concentrates on the tasks of divisional management. This last role choice sometimes serves as a strategic path of withdrawal for a division head trying to escape from the pressure toward political commitment.

While the task roles of division head and section head are rather clearly defined, this is not true of the subdivision head. His role is relatively new and his tasks are not clearly differentiated from those of the division head, a situation which some experience as a source of insecurity and others as a chance for shaping their role according to their own conceptions. [6]

While at the divisional level the "politician" is becoming gra-

81

dually the predominant or modal type, for most subdivision heads the "politician" is not a realistic role choice, notwithstanding isolated cases of political recruitment. Subdivision heads are at least one rank below "Ministerialdirektor" and enjoy the career civil servant's normal security of position, which militates against the recruitment of pronounced partisans. The major role alternatives for the subdivision head are therefore the "professional expert", the "non-partisan promotor", and the "subdivision administrator", with the choice depending largely on the way in which the division chief defines his role. The "professional expert" at the subdivision level is often found where the division chief is more the political type, especially where he lacks expertise in the division's substantive area of work. This combination seems to be particularly stable and effective. In extreme cases, however, the expert in the position of subdivision head is so strongly identified with the substantive work that his role shades into that of section head. Where the division head possesses professional expertise himself and plays the expert role, it is more difficult for a stable division of labor to evolve, and conflicts at the divisional leadership level are more likely.

In general it can be said that task role differentiation at the divisional leadership level is governed by the principle of complementarity: the subdivision heads concentrate more strongly on those functions from among the whole set to be fulfilled at this level which the division head himself is less interested in or less able to fulfill. Only in exceptional cases a second pattern of functional differentiation is found at the divisional level. Here the tasks of division and subdivision heads are not differentiated along functional lines but according to substantive areas, so that the officials at the divisional level form a team where all perform much the same functions, only with respect to different sets of programs.

The divisional leaders of a department rarely form a cohesive peer group. The major lines of communication within a department are vertical, and division heads compete with each other for executive attention, resources, and prestige. In practically all departments there exists a conference of division heads which is convened at regular intervals and often presided by the minister himself. But this body serves primarily as forum for exchanging information of more general interest and for settling administrative questions, instead of being a decision-making body where departmental policy is formulated. In fact, the departmental executive often prefers to deal with the individual division heads separately where divisional projects are at issue, not only for strategic reasons, but also because in many departments the subject matter with which the various divisions deal is too heterogeneous for them to have much substantive interests in common.

3.3 Policy-making functions of divisional leaders

With regard to participation in the substantive work of policy formation, the divisional leadership seems to play only a minor role at first sight. Policy initiatives originate very rarely at the divisional level proper. Moreover, only about half of the division and subdivision heads engage in the substantive work of preparing a program. A division chief does occasionally develop an initiative — as this has been defined above — in cases where a problem is politically too delicate or otherwise too "big" for the responsible section, or where the division head in question possesses some special competence and interest in the subject matter. Special competence and personal interest are also the main reasons for division and subdivision heads to participate actively in putting a program together, including the work of personally formulating all or at least larger portions of the text.

But there is more to policy formation than initiating a new project and preparing the text for parliamentary or executive approval. If judged by their engagement in these two specific categories of activities, the divisional leadership may not seem to be strongly involved in policy-making, and yet they are fully implicated in the total process — by providing substantive impulses for initiatives developed either at the level below or above, by repeatedly discussing projects in the phase of drafting with the responsible section, by screening section initiatives before passing them on, and by selectively promoting projects. The functions which the divisional leadership performs for policy-making are thus more of a mediating and integrating kind. There is a striking similarity here between the division of labor that obtains between sections and divisional leadership in the process of policy formation, and the differentiation found by Bower between the roles played by the operating units and divisional management in a large corporation, where the former define projects and the latter exert their influence by selectively sponsoring them, integrating through such selectivity the objectives of corporate policy with the chances for action perceived at the operating level. [7]

The special contribution of divisional leaders to policymaking derives primarily from their intermediate position in the departmental hierarchy, but is supported by two additional and interrelated organizational features: the lack of personal staff at the divisional level and the relatively small number of higher civil servants working in any one division or subdivision. The lack of personal staff may often be the reason why a division head provides policy impulses rather than developing divisional initiatives proper. The relatively small size of divisions — not only the small number of immediate subordinates, but of the total personnel responsibly engaged in developing programs — permits frequent personal contacts between sections and division or subdivision chiefs, so that the latter can easily remain quite fully informed of the progress of work on the various projects developed in the division. The divisional leadership has also an institutionalized safeguard of full information in the rule that all incoming mail (except for letters addressed personally to a subordinate) goes over the division (or subdivision) head's desk and is distributed from there to the sections. This can provide him with sufficient clues for asking questions where he really has not been informed of a possibly important matter.

In the iterative discussion process established between the two levels, the divisional leadership shapes the projects under development successively to fit the aims and overall strategy of the departmental executive. This mediating function in the process of policy formation obviously involves a certain amount of filtering. However, the continuous nature of the divisional leadership's influence on policy developed in the sections makes it often unnecessary to revert to an explicit rejection of inappropriate section initiatives. Theoretically section initiatives can be rejected and hence completely killed at the divisional level — something which is, incidentally, not possible in the case of documents prepared by the sections in response to a directive or request from the top; here the division head may at most insist on a reformulation, but may not keep back the matter altogether. But if a section initiative survives the prolonged discussion process — quite possibly at the price of a substantial modification of its content — it normally finds formal approval at the divisional level.

Filtering at the divisional level is of course a two-way process. There is not only the stream of documents moving upwards, which includes section requests, reports, answers to executive enquiries, and in general everthing which must be formally approved at a higher level. There is also the stream of communications moving in the opposite direction, which includes information, requests, and directives of the executive to be passed on to the sections, as well as all communications reaching them through formal channels from other divisions and other departments. It is interesting to note that the sections perceive less deliberate filtering by the divisional leadership in the downward than in the upward direction. The existing dissatisfaction with the information received from above and criticism of an insufficient specificity of top derectives are generally not attributed to any deliberate filtering by the divisional leadership. In contrast, the divisional leadership is seen to influence quite actively communications which are directed upwards or outwards. The form of such filtering varies, the most frequently practiced mode being to return a document to the responsible section head for revision after having discussed with him the changes which the division head thinks should be made. Only where this is not successful, a division head may decide to reject the proposal altogether, or to pass it on along with his explicit criticism or counter-proposal.

The mediating function of the divisional leadership is of crucial importance for the process of policy formation. This function can also be defined as the integration of politics with administration. More exactly, the divisional leaders have to articulate two sets of decision criteria with each other: those of technical knowledge and substantive expertise with those of political strategy. In the classical theory of bureaucracy, the institutional differentiation between parliament and bureaucracy was equated with the functional differentiation between politics and administration. But as the bureaucarcy itself becomes involved in policy-making, it is obvious that the re-integration of politics and administration must be effected at some point within the government organization. The minister is today primarily politician and can hardly be expected to perform this integrating function. The same tends to hold increasingly for the state secretaries, and in this measure the integrating or articulating function devolves upon the divisional leadership. To be able to perform this integrating function, divisional leaders must speak the language of the politician as well as of the bureaucrat, they must be men of two worlds as it were. What is so difficult about this is the need not only to understand the two "languages" oneself, but to be able to make the "pure" bureacrat and "pure" politician understand each other's point of view. This is in fact asking too much of many career civil servants and gives a distinct advantage to the external recruit with an unusual career, the marginal type with multiple reference groups — provided he is able to develop a second identity as a bureaucrat. If not, the outside recruit will fail as well. He will not get his division to produce what he asks of it (and may have to sit down and do it himself) and/or he may not be able to make the executive see the point of divisional proposals. The problem, incidentally, is not peculiar to the specific case at hand. It can be said generally that roles with liaison or articulation functions grow in importance with increasing functional differentiation and professional specialization, though by the same token they may be increasingly difficult to fill.

4. Executive organization

A prominent feature of the still prevailing type of departmental organization is the relatively small institutional capacity at the top. The departmental executive includes the minister and the state secretaries. The minister is traditionally aided by a personal assistant, usually a younger civil servant; by a small bureau (*Ministerbüro*) taking care of more routine clerical and administrative tasks; by a press and/or public relations assistant; and by a small office (or an officer) for cabinet and parliamentary matters. The state secretaries have usually only one personal assistant and a secretary, but no further staff. Thus staff help at the top has been traditionally very limited.

This traditional form of executive organization is the institutional reflection of a highly personalized and functionally restricted conception of executive control. The small ministerial staff is mostly a personal task force of the minister, having been selected by him and prepared to leave office when he does. This degree of personal dependence on the minister would be impossible if the staff were large and permanent. The small personal staff thus maximizes trust and personal loyalty. Its smallness, on the other hand, is no drawback if the minister is not expected to control the department and its operation fully and systematically. Of the two major aspects of executive control — control of the "production" process or of the so-called goal activities, and control of the producing system (the classical O&M functions) — the minister has traditionally been expected to restrict himself mainly to the first. The classical functions of organization and management were institutionalized in the matrix structure of division Z, which has been described in the first section of this chapter. This structure was designed to make the continuous operation of the department independent of executive control. But even with respect to the control of the substance of departmental "production" the demands traditionally made on the minister were limited, since until recently the bureaucracy was less involved in planning and since the basic operating units have always been expected to work rather independently in their defined area of responsibility.

As departments grow in size and especially as the demands in the area of planning increase significantly, the traditional type of executive organization proves to be inadequate because it prevents the commensurate extension of the departmental executive's directive capacity. The needs of crisis management and the tasks deriving from the political aspects of the departmental executive's role take up so much time that without help of a larger top level staff, planning functions often remain unfulfilled. Instead of systematic and long-range policy planning the executive overwhelmingly engages only in some sort of time budgeting for major departmental activities, and not even this much is found in all departments.

The prevailing organizational response to these recognized shortcomings has been a limited expansion by adding personnel but without changing the structure of executive organization basically. Thus the number of state secretaries has grown, and instead of one public relations assistant there may now be a staff of two or three. Only rarely have new staff units been created for new functions connected with planning. However, there have been some changes in the departmental organization below the executive level which were designed to increase the departmental capacity for planning; to these structural reforms we will turn in chapter VII.

4.1 Executive roles

In the early years of the Federal Republic, most departments had only one permanent secretary, who was a career civil servant normally promoted from among the department's group of division heads. This permanent secretary constituted an important element of continuity at the top since he usually remained in office longer than a minister. At first a growing number of departments started to have two instead of one permanent secretary. In 1967 an additional type of executive role was created, the parliamentary secretary (*Parlamentarischer Staatssekretär*). [8] This new type of state secretary was explicitly meant to be recruited according to criteria of political affiliation. He has to be a member of parliament and is often a man of the minister's personal confidence; it happens, however, that a parliamentary secretary of another coalition party is appointed in order to provide a degree of political balance or even to keep watch over a particular minister. The parliamentary secretary's term of office is restricted to the legislative period. His major function is officially to strengthen the department's relations to the political bodies — parties, parliamentary party groups, and *Bundesrat* — , while he is not supposed to devote himself to departmental administration. The addition of the parliamentray secretary brought the number of state secretaries up to three in some ministries. The Minister of Finance who took office in 1972 has been the first to insist on having two parliamentary secretaries and thus four state secretaries in all.

The intended task differentiation between the two types of state secretary corresponds to the traditional distinction between the non-partisan civil servant and the political leader. However, as mentioned before, the tenured permanent secretary has also become defined as a "political civil servant" and is increasingly being recruited from the outside and according to political criteria. As a consequence there exist no standardized roles for the two types of state secretary which would hold for all departments. There is as much varietty in actual role performance and in the evolving patterns of task differentiation at the level of the state secretaries as was previously shown to exist at the divisional leaderhip level.

Among the roles actually played by state secretaries we find the same four types already described in the previous section, though with certain modifications which are due to the difference in organizational level. Beginning with the three variants of the "bureaucrat" role, the state secretary who chooses the "administrator" role acts as manager for the whole department, which means that he is responsible for the administrative and managerial tasks located in division Z — personnel, organization, budgeting and accounting, and householding functions such as building maintenance, car pool, technical services etc. This role is mainly played by the non-partisan, career civil servant advancing to permanent secretary. There are cases where division Z is directly subordinate to the parliamentary secretary, but he rarely plays this particular role exclusively.

If a state secretary plays the role of "professional expert", he engages actively in program development, discussing substantive questions in detail with the responsible section and division heads, while de-emphasizing the more formal tasks of planning and coordinating divisional activities. This is a likely role choice for professionals recruited from outside the career civil service and is rarely found among either career bureaucrats and parliamentary secretaries.

In contrast, the role of "promotor" can be played by permanent as well as parliamentary secretaries. However, at the departmental level this role requires not only political skills but also some political power and is therefore difficult to play for a strictly non-partisan civil servant. At the departmental level the promotor role thus shades easily into that of "politician". An interesting mixture of the two types is found where a state secretary possesses specialized professional competence in one particular area of the department's activities and attempts, by selectively promoting departmental project in this area, to further his political career as he styles himself to be the party's expert in that field.

The role of "politician" is played mostly by parliamentary secretaries, though by no means all of them could be thus classified. In the pure case, the "politician" has little substantive interest in any particular policy field and little professional expertise. He is a generalized promotor, sponsoring projects which he expects to become political assets for his party or his minister, always intent to enhance the power position and slate of "successes" of his party, his minister, and himself.

Among the several state secretaries within one department there usually evolves some pattern of task differentiation. A very successful combination is that between permanent secretaries playing the role of "professional expert", and parliamentary secretaries combining the roles of promotor and politician. It cannot be said generally who should play the role of departmental administrator. The permanent secretary might easily perform the corresponding functions without considering their interdependence with policy, and politics, while the parliamentary secretary who assumes this role in addition to that of promotor and/or politician is easily overburdened.

The top role in an organization is very often formally the least structured one. This is certainly true for the role of federal minister. His behavior is influenced more by situational constraints and political exigencies than by explicit and formal role expectations. This gives him considerable leeway in interpreting his role, including his relations with the state secretaries. It is partly the size and composition of a department, and partly the minister's personal leadership style which determine whether the nucleus of executive organization has a more hierarchical or more group-like, even team-like structure. Team-like here means that the minister and his state secretaries constitute in fact but one hierarchical level and that major questions are discussed and important decisions made jointly. This structural pattern evolves most easily in small and homogeneous departments. In the case of a hierarchical structuring at the top the state secretaries are responsible for different divisions and report to the minister within their specified task area. Large departments with a correspondingly high demand for executive action, especially if they are composed of divisions dealing with rather heterogenous matters requiring specialized leadership attention, seem to tend toward this structural pattern at the top. In this case the state secretaries constitute a hierarchical level between the division chiefs and the minister. There may even be an internal differentiation of rank among the state secretaries, so that one of them serves as superordinate coordinator and has the most direct and most frequent contact with the minister. This easily follows from the greater demand for coordination which arises with specializtion at the level of state secretaries.

4.2 Executive functions in policy-making

As has been shown, the institutionalized capacity for planning within the traditional and still prevailing type of executive organization is extremely small. It is therefore a question to what extent the departmental executive can fully and systematically control the formation of departmental policy, either by initiating policy centrally and/or by directing the decentralized development of policy in the basic operating units.

Due to the limited capacity at the top and the confluence of a multitude of diverse and pressing demands, executive attention is one of the scarcest resources in the department. Inevitably, executive attention is allocated selectively. This would even be true if executive capacity were less restricted than it is under the organizational conditions described above; even then executive attention could not be given continuously and evenly to *all* policy formation processes within the department. The problem has therefore a qualitative as well as a quantitative aspect, i.e. it is not only the question how much executive attention is restricted, but also whether the criteria of selective allocation of attention are "rational" with respect to the fulfillment of the executive functions in policy-making.

The informally operating rules for the selective allocation of executive attention can be formulated roughly as follows. (1) Executive attention is allocated to politically controversial problems and to policy initiatives which are likely to trigger intense political conflict. (2) Executive attention is given to projects and proposals which serve the management of an acute crisis. (3) Selective attention is paid to the development of programs which are likely to receive wide publicity and to gain public acclaim. (4) Executive attention is given to issues which have provoked public criticism of the department and to cases where the department has bungled something visibly. (5) Attention must be given to matters brought forth by another cabinet member, a member of the executive's party group, or some other politically important person. (6) Finally, executives normally develop personal interest in specific matters or in some specified policy field; these interests are often biographically determined and channel executive attention selectively.

The aggregate outcome of these implicit rules for the allocation of executive attention is often a seemingly irrational pattern: apparently minor questions receive pronounced attention and are followed closely by the executive, while programs with important long-range impacts clamour for attention in vain. Occasionally the combination of extreme pressure (high demand for attention) and lack of a *systematic* selectivity may in fact produce true irrationalities. More often the irrationality is only apparent; what is really involved is simply a different set of rationality criteria. The departmental executive, and in particular the minister, is constrained to orient his actions at the needs of political survival; to this end he must avoid loosing support and attempt to collect visible success for himself, his party, and the government. Actions which serve these goals are rational for the departmental executive, and they are not less so because theirs is a political rationality. In content, however, the criteria of political rationality are different from the criteria which define the efficient fulfillment of any of the intra-organizational functions, and also from the criteria which define the substantive rationality of a policy decision. As politician and department head the departmental executive is therefore in principle exposed to the claims of several different sets of rationality criteria. But in practice ministers and at least those state secretaries who define their role in political terms tend to give priority to the criteria of political rationality. In this they differ from the divisional leaders, who face basically the same situation but are constrained to articulate the different sets of rationality criteria with each other.

The lack of an institutionalized capacity for policy planning at the top, combined with the politically motivated selectivity in the allocation of executive attention, explain why the departmental executive does not direct the policy making process by systematically developing those initiatives which are the substance of an active policy. Centrally initiated programs are relatively rare. In fact we already pointed out that the majority of policy initiatives originate at the section level. In qualitative terms, those policy initiatives which do originate at the top of the department reflect the operation of the selective criteria just discussed.

The last point needs to be elaborated. It will be remembered that due to the structural constraints described in part 2 of this chapter, section initiatives tend to be short-range in time perspective, restricted in scope, and incremental in nature. These characteristics of reactive rather than active policy-making are not basically different where decentral initiatives are developed by several sections in a pattern of horizontal self-coordination. On the other hand, policy initiatives which are long-range in time perspective, of broad scope, and deal with controversial questions, are usually of central origin. If one traces the genesis of those policy decisions made in the past few years which possess these characteristics of an active policy, they are found to originate quite often within the political executive (cabinet) or parliament. Of course, it is possible that programs initiated by statements made in the chancellor's government declaration or commissioned by parliament go back to impulses coming from within the departments. But without explicit support by the political executive and/or parliament these impulses would not have become policy initiatives, so that they are justly classified as of central origin.

If the greater chances for initiating active policy which obviously exist at the top were systematically utilized, there would be complementarity between centralized and decentralized policy initiation and neither the "small" nor the "big" problems would be neglected. But to this end central initiatives would have to be the result of a *systematic* search (a) for problems which fall in between the defined areas of responsibility of the sections and are not approached for that reason, and (b) for problems which are not made the object of section initiatives because they are too large of scope or politically too controversial. This, however, is not the case: central initiatives are rarely the result of such systematic search processes, and this is not only due to the insufficient scanning and information processing capacity at the top, but also to the observed selectivity in the allocation of executive attention.

Executive control of policy-making does of course not depend on central initiation. Current management theory considers goal setting as the prime leadership function and makes a clear distinction between the production process itself, and its direction and control. Applied to the federal ministries one could consequently argue that the departmental executive need not, or even that it ought not to initiate policy, much less engage in the substantive work of developing programs. All it should do is to direct the policy-making process by formulating explicit policy goals as guidelines for decentral initiatives, and by exerting its influence through repeated interventions in on-going processes of decentralized program development. In fact, however, this form of executive control of policy-making is not very pronounced either. There are hardly any instances where the departmental executive formulates explicitly policy directives which could serve as *general* orientation for the decentral initiation and elaboration of policy. *Specific* policy directives from the executive are tantamount to central initiatives and are interpreted and acted upon accordingly. But as far as general guidelines for policy-making are concerned, the bureaucracy must largely try to infer these.

The extent to which the departmental executive participates in on-going processes of program development depends again on the selective allocation of executive attention. Whether "small" or "big", centrally or decentrally initiated — if a program meets the criteria of executive attention the minister himself may intervene in the process of drafting and will comment in detail on proposals formally submitted to him. Whether he is able to suggest modifications or alternatives depends, of course, on his own professional expertise. Where the minister lacks the knowledge for a critical evaluation of substantive details, his comments may be limited to questions about consequences, cautionary remarks, reminders of political constraints etc. This may not be enough to give substantive guidance, but it does amount to an effort to control aspects of the project which are politically relevant. The same holds for the state secretaries. In contrast, matters which fail to receive substantial executive attention because none of the criteria of selective interest define them as important can be largely pursued by the subordinate units without executive intervention, up to the point where the final decision has to be made. This means that in such cases, no matter how important they may be according to the criteria of an active policy, little guidance is forthcoming from the top.

If we measure the practice of executive control against certain expectations derived from management theory, we must conclude that the departmental executive does not fully and systematically control the formation of departmental policy. But this is not the whole story. In spite of unquestionable deficiencies in the directive capacity of the departmental executive, it would be wrong to conclude that the federal bureaucracy operates more or less independently of executive control. This will become clearer as we consider in the following chapter the aggregate effect on policy-making of the structural features described in this chapter.

Chapter VI

THE PROCESS
OF POLICY-MAKING

1. The federal bureaucracy — self-controlling?

From the description of sectional activities, divisional leadership, and executive control there emerges a pattern which evokes at first sight the classical theory of Max Weber that the bureaucratic staff tends to emancipate itself from the political leadership and to become self-controlling, or even able to manipulate its leaders. Weber's crucial premise was that in the bureaucratic form of organization, authority must rest on expert knowledge, and that the monopoly which bureaucrats have on expert knowledge gives them the chance to emancipate themselves from their political masters. But looking more closely it becomes evident that the classical theory of bureaucracy does not fit our facts.

To begin with, the federal bureaucracy does not attempt actively to circumvent executive control and to impose upon the political executive a course of action developed according to its own preferences. On the contrary, section and division heads generally try to avoid developing initiatives and making proposals which they know to deviate from the political executive's intentions. Occasionally such deviating proposals are made for strategic reasons, to test whether a change of opinion at the top is possible or to provoke a revision of existing views. But there is no intention in these cases to force the minister's hand and his negative reaction is respected. It needs the relatively rare case of the emphatically non-political (not only non-partisan!) professional for deviant initiatives consciously to be started out of the conviction to 'know better'.

There are, of course, indirect ways to influence the departmental leadership. It may in fact be difficult for the executive to evaluate proposals critically for lack of relevant expert knowledge; this is the way how staff experts generally influence the decision of line superiors. It is also possible to build up support for some proposal before submitting it to the executive. If the initiating unit succeeds to involve other departments (at the section or divisional level) and/or external organizations interested in the matter and to negotiate a jointly acceptable draft proposal with them before formally submitting it to the departmental executive, the minister may find it very difficult to say No. Such strategies are doubtlessly used from time to time with the intention of influencing the executive's decision. But this is not the rule. Normally the minister will be informed that an agreement is being negotiated with another department, so that he has the chance to intervene if he so wishes.

The federal bureaucracy seems generally to make little use of the strategy of withholding information, which would be another indirect way of diminishing effective executive control. Superordinates at the divisional or top level do not complain that relevant information is wilfully kept black by their subordinates and attribute informational deficiencies to objective reasons such as lack of time or the insufficient quality of the information gathering system. Existing formal rules which specify what is to be reported upwards are generally observed, and there is a tendency to interpret such rules widely rather than narrowly, i.e. to report upwards or pass on up for decision even more than would be necessary according to the rules.

Federal bureaucrats are quite willing to accept executive directives and to act upon them. Such compliance is not unconditional, but the condition is not that the departmental executive is legitimated by superior professional competence. On the contrary, the political basis of the minister's authority is recognized; the same holds for politically recruited state secretaries. However, the political executive is expected to recognize the limitations of its knowledge and to listen to the arguments of the professionals, even if it does not follow their proposals. Should a minister simply ignore the reasoned opinion of his department, he would meet with passive resistance instead of willing compliance.

Attitudinal factors are partly responsible for the willingness to accept executive directives. It is the civil servants' overwhelmingly positive attitude toward the present political, social, and economic system in the German Federal Republic which makes them accept the political basis of the executive's authority. Needless to say, the long period of uninterrupted majority rule by the Christian Democrats also led to the development of a specially pronounced, substantive consensus among politicians and senior civil servants. When the Social Democrats came to power, there were some politically motivated attempts to evade executive control. But even then this tendency did not assume threatening proportions, partly because of the countervailing force of the civil servant's role definition as politically sensitive, but non-partisan expert, which still prevails below the level of divisional leadership.

We must conclude that it is not the result of a pronounced tendency on the part of the bureaucracy to evade executive control and become self-controlling if much policy is initiated decentrally and if the executive does not direct this process systematically by formulating explicit policy goals and closely controlling the decentral development of new programs. This conclusion poses two new problems. If the bureaucracy is so willing to accept executive control of policy-making, is reference to the small institutionalized working capacity at the top really a sufficient explanation for the observed control deficiencies? Why, in particular, does the executive fail to guide decentral policy-making by systematically formulating explicit policy goals? And secondly, what happens if not enough executive directives are forthcoming to provide guidance for the sections in program initiation and development — does the bureaucracy become self-controlling against its own compliant inclinations, or how else does it fill the apparent void? In the attempt to answer these questions it will be discovered that executive control is in fact less deficient than it has so far appeared to be, because there is a good deal of indirect and not easily recognizable control taking place.

2. The control problem in policy-making

To understand this evolving pattern of control, it is necessary to begin by considering the nature of the control problem with which the departmental executive is faced in the area of policy development.

The standard types of direction, or models of management, are all based on some form of task differentiation between top and bottom along the dimension leadership—production. Of these models of management none really fits the case of the ministries.

It is obvious that policy-making is an activity which cannot be highly routinized, i.e. directed by generalized rules and conditional programs of the 'if—then' type, except in procedural aspects. This largely precludes also the so-called management by exception, because the 'exception' would sooner be the rule. On the other hand the leadership cannot direct all or even most activities ad hoc, which is true of all large organizations. It may seem that management by objectives provides a suitable model. The leadership would formulate policy goals ('objectives') and the subunits in the departments would be expected to choose the right path towards the attainment of these goals, i.e. develop corresponding programs. On closer inspection, however, this model cannot be applied to the federal ministries either.

To the extent that the ministries develop policy which must subsequently be approved by the cabinet and/or parliament, they fulfill a staff function. For this particular function the distinction between goal setting and implementation becomes tenuous. There are, of course, also implementative activities being performed by the lower ranks in the ministries. The production of booklets, films, and other information material by the Press Office can for instance be considered as implementation of previously set public relations goals. In this case performance could in principle be controlled by evaluating it against objectives. The control problem for the process of policy formation is of an entirely different nature. The sections and divisions do not *implement* objectives set by the political executive when they develop policy initiatives and draft programs, they rather *produce* them. A precisely formulated policy goal is not very different from a policy initiative. Any general policy objective, as for instance 'quality of life', is highly diffuse and leaves enormously wide margins for interpretation. To fulfill a directive function, policy goals must be more specific. It is extremely difficult, however, to formulate policy goals which are sufficiently specific to provide orientation for the sections and to serve as evaluating criteria for policy proposals developed by them — but are not yet such proposals themselves. This means that the management functions of goal setting and control cannot be clearly separated from the 'production' process itself where policy is the product. Nor is this an abstract argument referring merely to an analytical distinction. It means that in practice the wonted division of labor between top and bottom tends to disappear. And in fact one gets the impression that in the federal departments all hierarchial levels are doing qualitatively more or less the same thing with respect to policy-making, except that they do it on the basis of different sets of information, with a different breadth of horizon, and with different decision criteria.

The basic difficulty in developing policy directives is that as general goals are operationalized, they shade into specific proposals. But specific proposals cannot be formulated by the top alone, for lack of the requisite knowledge. The specific formulation of policy requires not only instrumental knowledge of available alternatives for the solution of a problem. The scope for a voluntaristic choice of specific policy goals is also severely restricted by the need to respond to an uncontrollable variety of environmental inputs which the political system cannot afford to ignore, as well as by numerous constraints, including existing commitments, scarce resources, and side-effects which must be avoided. Neither the instrumental (or professional) knowledge nor the knowledge of these constraints is fully present at the top. Such knowledge is primarily possessed by the basic operating units. The sections are staffed with experienced professionals, and they function as sensors of the policy-making system. By following intensively the developments in their respective sectors of the environment, they perceive existing problems and conceive of possibilities for their solution. The sections must therefore contribute their detailed knowledge of existing constraints and of the chances for action to the formulation of policy goals. For this reason it is not to be expected that the departmental executive controls policy-making systematically by formulating policy objectives voluntaristically. A 'topdown' process of policy-making where the sections derive specific programs deductively from general policy goals defined at the top is practically impossible, and undesirable too.

It would of course be wrong to conclude that, since the 'top-down' model of policy-making is not a valid prescription, the process of policy-making should follow a 'bottom-up' model instead. In such a model the departmental executive would not attempt to formulate general policy goals, but controls program content by selecting, according to its own political criteria, the best alternatives from among those passed up to it from below. Here the executive has theoretically the full sway of action possibilities to choose from, provided that no information processing (i.e., evaluation of observed constraints and action possibilities and condensation into a few proposals) occurs on the way from the sections to the top. This, however, would mean to abolish all division of labor in the decision-making process and would lead to a fatal information overload at the top.

3. The dialogue model

The control model which is adequate to the needs of policy-making is neither a top-down nor a bottom-up model, but one which provides for the integration of the top-down and bottom-up processes. This is a complex model of an iterative process where the directives coming from the top are informed by the perceptions of problems, possible solutions, and situational constraints coming from below, and where these directives in turn structure perceptions and the search for solutions at the section level. This 'dialogue model' of policy-making does involve a division of labor between the levels, even if not in terms of a clear-cut distinction between goal-setting and implementation in the 'production' of policy. Task differentiation between levels rather refers to the processing of information, which is governed by different criteria.

Elements of such a pattern can be found in the federal departments. The different organizational levels are involved in a permanent discussion with each other, though this discussion remains partly implicit. As we proceed to look more closely at this peculiar dialogue, we shall also recognize in it a mechanism of indirect executive control over the decentralized development of policy.

We have seen why it is difficult to formulate systematically central directives which are both general and operational and could instruct the sections in the decentral initiation of policy, providing them with criteria which tell when a program change or a new program is needed. Where such central directives do not exist, the sections will define in various ways their own criteria for deciding whether and what kind of a policy initiative is needed. Two predominant substitute orientations are professional convictions and clientèle interests. In the first case shared norms and situational interpretations which are current in the relevant profession may provide impulses for action. This mode of orientation is found especially among persons with a training in one of the technical professions or a natural science, and generally more among non-jurists than jurists. In the case of a clientele orientation the impulses defining the situation as in need for a change come from the groups affected by current policy in the area, who make specific criticisms or specific demands.

These impulses then pass through the filter of selective criteria described in section 2 of the previous chapter. It will be remembered that these criteria refer in part to the perceived chance of success for a given initiative. After all, even programs and projects which lie outside the focus of executive attention must be submitted to it for final approval. The chances for success are low where top level support cannot be gained for a project, and swimming against the stream of executive opinion may be costly in terms of one's own career. Realizing this, and generally not being much inclined to escape executive control, the subordinate ranks attempt to anticipate executive reactions to the projects they seem to develop without intervention and guidance from the top. If a clientèle oriented section head is convinced for instance that the minister would not be prepared to satisfy the demands of a particular clientèle group, the criterion of success militates against an initiative in favor of these demands. The anticipation of executive reactions by the section personnel brings the executive into a kind of vicarious exchange of views with the department's social environment. For the sections the anticipation of executive reactions means that their margin for self-direction is in fact rather strictly bounded by a self-imposed discipline, which might be expressed in the implicit maxim: develop your own ideas, but in doing so do not deviate from executive intentions.

To be able to anticipate executive reactions to their proposals where they cannot refer to explicit directives, officials try their best to inform themselves in other ways of the executive's intentions, wishes, and opinions. They carefully read public speeches and published interviews of the minister and the state secretaries, and analyze every incidental remark they make. Important sources of orientation are the programmatic pronouncements made in the government declaration at the beginning of the new legislative period, and official reports which a number of ministries prepare to document their achievements and state future aims. Of course, official reports, speeches, interviews, and incidental remarks are not made with the intention of guiding the work of the sections within the department, which can make it difficult to infer the executive's true intentions correctly. Sometimes more direct attempts to precipitate a specific reaction are made by launching 'test balloons', preferably as oral proposals or direct questions, but since section heads do not often meet the executive personally, also in written form.

The fact that executive intentions are often not known to the lower levels does not mean that the political executive deliberately keeps its views and intentions secret. This is rarely the case. Much more frequently the executive has no specific intentions ex ante, but these are generated ad hoc only when it is confronted with a specific proposal for action. To stimulate the political executive to form opinions on specific matters is part of the role the sections must play if the dialogue model of policy-making is to function.

A certain weakness of the dialogue as it actually operates in the federal departments lies in its largely implicit nature, which is connected with the fact that the dialogue must take place within the framework of a hierarchial organization which does not provide enough institutionalized occasions for discussion between the ranks. But the crucial weakness of the actual dialogue lies in the selectivity which characterizes the process of upward communication, and which is a lower level reaction to the perceived selectivity in the allocation of executive attention.

We already mentioned in the previous chapter that the sections are quite willing to inform their superiors well about their activities and plans. In practically all departments there exist more or less elaborate sets of general rules and specific directives about the information of the executive by the sections and the divisional leadership. Some rules are also contained in the Joint Manual of Procedure referred to earlier. These rules or directives usually specify rather clearly certain kinds of events to be reported (for instance all contacts with members of parliament, meetings with representatives of certain interest organizations etc.), or they name particular extra-departmental senders whose wishes or opinions are to be passed upwards. Such rules are unequivocal and easy to comply with. The same is true where certain matters are subject to final approval at a given hierarchial level. However, responsibilities are not fixed by rules for all conceivable matters. Where the hierarchical location of responsibility is not explicitly set down, it depends on the importance of a matter who is to make the decision. Accordingly the rules about upward information often speak of 'questions of fundamental importance', 'matters of political relevance', or some such vague category of information content, that must be submitted to the executive. This general vagueness in specifying by *content* the information to be passed upwards is not the result of simple negligence. The problem of formulating rules for upward information is structurally analogous to the problem of formulating directives for policy-making. As a matter of fact, existing information rules which contain an operational criterion such as a certain category of senders, or events, are not infrequently criticized by the ministerial personnel, because these criteria are not correlated closely enough with the relative importance of the information content and oblige them occasionally to report trifles.

102

The absence of operational criteria for what is 'important' or 'politically relevant' forces the lower ranks to decide this by themselves. Since the importance of some item of information is often established only by the course of subsequent events, there is a spontaneous inclination to communicate too much rather than too little in order to be on the safe side. But it may be disadvantageous to create the impression among one's superiors of being unable to tell the important from the unimportant and to be afraid of acting on one's own initiative. It is therefore necessary to infer what *the executive* might think is important for it to know, and this corresponds roughly to the previously described pattern of selective attention. The departmental executive is thus informed about impending crises, about events likely to be taken up by one of the political bodies (from party to parliament) or by the mass media, and about matters which are likely to arouse conflicts the executive will eventually have to solve. A state secretary who is known to be particularly interested in, say, questions of food and drug control receives full and timely information about developments and possible initiatives in this area. The minister and the parliamentary secretary will also be informed in detail about matters concerning their constituencies and about matters concerning specific social groups for which they serve as advocates. In this way what is communicated upwards is structured by the perceived selectivity of executive attention, and since this is primarily geared to the exigencies of political survival, the resulting information basis at the top is an insufficient foundation for systematic policy planning. Its very selectivity does not permit even the reactive development of directives for policy-making in all of the department's areas of responsibility. An enlarged information processing capacity at the top could break up this vicious circle, though this measure by itself certainly would not guarantee a functioning 'dialogue' process of policy-making.

In a number of departments attempts have recently been made to avoid the incompleteness of the traditional pattern by formalizing the process of upward communication in such a way as to guarantee broad and continuous information. In one department the executive keeps a file of all current projects which is periodically being updated. Other departments use weekly reports to be delivered by all divisions. But these and other institutionalized procedures are to no avail if information processing capacity at the top is insufficient to make use of the information collected. The reporting units notice this quickly and stop making a serious effort to be exact, complete, and regular in reporting.

A crucial link in a functioning 'dialogue' between executive and operating units is the divisional leadership; this is in fact the context in which its previously described mediating function must be seen. The (reactively of independently formed) directives of the executive cannot be sufficiently specific to shape a developing policy initiative or project according to its intentions, unless the executive is informed of the problem and the contemplated solution early enough and in sufficient detail. This poses an obvious problem in view of the large number of projects being pursued in a department at the same time. The divisional leadership must therefore filter and condense the upward stream of communication so that the amount reaching the top is manageable, but sufficient as information basis for policy planning and direction. At the same time it must serve a translator and amplifier function in the downward process of communication, interpreting general executive directives in the context of specific problems.

The successful performance of the divisional leadership's mediating role in the dialogue between executive and operating units depends mainly on three conditions. The divisional leadership must first of all be fully informed of sectional activities. We have already noted that this is usually the case. Secondly the divisional leadership must be informed of the strategic goals and political constraints at the top. Only this enables it to judge the 'importance' or 'political relevance' of a given matter with more certainty than a section head can do, and filter upward communication accordingly. To be able to 'translate' political constraints and general policy directives into the concrete details of program decisions the divisional leadership must finally possess substantive expertise. This condition is mostly, but not generally fulfilled.

The main weakness in the way in which the divisional leadership plays its part in the discussion process between top and bottom lies in the repetition at this level of the already noted selectivity in upward communication. A divisional leadership which transmits to the departmental executive not simply what it asks for but what it would need for a more systematic direction of major policy developments, could within limits off-set the deleterious effects of selective executive interest and of the reactive selectivity of communications from the sections. Undoubtedly there are division heads who know what they want the minister to pay attention to, and orient their informational behavior accordingly. This, however, will not be systematic, but selective in its own way. A predominant tendency is for the divisional leadership to pass upwards what it anticipates will meet the executive's criteria of importance — aside from information which the rules call for or which the executive specificially requests. In this way the deficiencies already noted in the vertical communication process are reinforced at the middle level.

We can conclude that while certain prerequisites for a functioning dialogue between the levels in the process of policy-making are fulfilled, the model is not optimally developed in the present operation of the federal departments. The departmental structure and the existing communication patterns between the levels are not well adapted to the needs of the dialogue. However, the road toward a possible reform lies in improving the dialogue, and not in attempts to introduce a more hierarchial, top-down model of executive control over policy-making.

Chapter VII

STRUCTURAL REFORMS: ORGANIZATION FOR PLANNING

When the need for planned and active policy-making became pressing in the sixties, the political leadership responded with efforts to adapt the governmental organization to the new demands. Beginning in the middle of the decade and increasing sharply when the Social-Liberal coalition took office, the formerly hostile attitude of the government toward planning was replaced by a positive attitude which at times even grew into a planning euphoria. This change in orientation was reflected in procedural and structural innovations both at the departmental and at the cabinet, or top political, level. Some of these innovations have already been mentioned, such as the establishment of project groups and attempts to adapt the size and structure of the permanent operating units of departmental organization to the new functional requirements. Improvements were also made in the system of information gathering and processing; to the extent that they involve the bureaucracy itself, these will briefly be discussed in the following chapter. In this chapter we shall first turn to innovations in the departmental organization for planning and subsequently to some relevant reform efforts at the top political level.

1. Departmental organization for planning

A number of efforts have been made since the middle of the sixties in order to adapt the departmental organization to the tasks

107

of planning. Most of the organizational changes introduced to this effect involve the creation of new staff or line units with special functions in the area of planning.

In addition, in 1970 every department appointed a planning commissioner upon request of the Chancellor's Office. Generally of the rank of division head, the structural location of this official differs between departments. His main functions lie in the area of interdepartmental coordination and in managing the collection of departmental information about on-going policy developments for the Chancellor's Office. The planning commissioner is thus a part of the government-wide planning system, rather than representing a departmental reform effort. [1]

Recently first attempts have been made to restructure the traditional departmental line organization according to program categories, mainly by reshuffling assignments between sections and divisions. The first specific proposal to this effect has been developed with the assistance of a management consulting firm for the Department of Agriculture, where it is to be introduced for a test period. [2] The effects of the reorganization remain to be seen.

The following discussion must therefore be limited to the new departmental planning units, which can be classified by the function they fulfill and by their organizational location. We distinguish the following three functional types:

(1) Units which assist the executive in directing the process of policy-making within the department. Orienting their work directly toward the needs of the top executive, the major dimension of communication for this type of unit is vertical. Horizontal relations to the divisions are typically weak.

(2) Units which direct and coordinate the process of program development within the department. These units cooperate systematically and directly with the divisions, whose work they are supposed to structure in a certain direction. In this case it is the horizontal dimension of interaction which predominates.

(3) Units which themselves engage in planning, i.e. which develop programs and policy in lieu of the divisions.

By organizational location we can distinguish staff from line units. Staff units are directly subordinate to the top executive, while line units would be located within the divisional structure. Such a line unit may be an entire division, a subdivision, or simply a section. There is no logically necessary relationship between the types of function and the organizational location of a unit. Empirically, however, staff location is the exception rather than the rule among the newly created special units.

108

1.1 Units supporting the executive

Units with a predominantly supportive function (type 1) are virtually the only ones which are located as top level staffs. Such a staff unit exists for instance in the Department of Housing and Urban Affairs; together with the staff units for cabinet and parliamentary matters and for public relations this small planning unit is directly subordinate to the top executive. At the time of our investigation this unit was practically a one man staff. It followed the development of such programs in other departments which had consequences for urban development and assisted the minister in defining his position when such a program was presented to the cabinet for decision. It also gathered information for the executive about the major program developments going on within the department. This staff unit was much too small to engage in attempts to coordinate, much less to direct the work of the divisions. It communicated rarely with the divisions directly, but did so frequently with the top executive. Considerable influence was therefore attributed to the planning staff by the department's line units, which tended to resent this influence in direct measure to their own lack of contact with the staff.

Staff location is, however, not the rule among units which perform supportive functions for the top executive. Within the division Z of the Ministry of the Interior there exists for instance one section which is formally subordinate to the divisional leadership, but works in fact directly for the top executive. At the time of our investigation, this section, too, had only irregular contacts with other line units in the department. It did not follow the process of program development within the department, since it lacked capacity for this job. Its supportive function for the top executive was primarily of a political nature. The executive occasionally asked this section to help some other section or division in working out a determinate project or proposal — not in order to increase its capacity but to make sure that the executive's political goals were sufficiently taken into account. The section also observed the policies of departments controlled by the coalition partner in so far as they touched upon certain substantive areas in which the minister's own political party had a particular interest. In a way this unit can therefore be described as a staff which serves the top executive as look-out post and occasional task force.

1.2 Units with directive functions

In the federal ministries no top level staff units have been created which fulfill *more* than supportive functions for the departmental executive. This means that none of the newly created units engaged in planning (functions of type 2 and 3) is located as a top level staff. On the other hand there is a great diversity of line units with planning functions. Where these functions are to be performed for the whole department, the planning units have generally the status of a subdivision or even division.

Some newly created planning units of type 2 do not serve the whole department but have a more specialized and restricted competence. An example is the newly created subdivision within the Ministry of the Interior's division for environmental protection. It grew out of a former section which fulfilled coordinating functions in the development of the federal government's program for the protection of the environment. The rapid rise of interest in questions of pollution, waste disposal, and the conservation of the eco-system, called for an integration and expansion of the formerly rather isolated and dispersed federal activities in this area. It became the special task of the new subdivision to direct the work of the other sections in such a way that they took account of the new, "integrated" perspective and produced together something like a coherent environmental policy. Within the Department of the Interior, of course, environmental protection is but one of several areas of policy-making.

An example of a planning unit designed to direct and coordinate all major policy-making activities of a whole department is the planning division in the Ministry of Labor and Social Affairs. The example is particularly instructive because after initial difficulties this planning division became quite effective, which permits the identification of certain structural prerequisites for the successful fulfillment of the directive function.

The planning division in the Ministry of Labor has four subdivisions. Two of the subdivisions are supposed to control the development of policy initiatives in the other divisions by checking whether they are in agreement with the department's general political orientation, whether they are financially sound and realistic, and what their economic consequences would be. This means that the planning division through two of its subunits is supposed to serve a function of selective reinforcement in the process of policy-making, but normally it does not initiate policy itself. At the

110

same time the planning division is expected to coordinate the various processes of policy development within the department both substantively and in terms of time scheduling. Coordination of departmental activities at least in the sense of time scheduling is an important function of directive units wherever these are found.

The other two subdivisions of the planning division fulfill supportive functions for the rest of the department. Thus all statictical, mathematical, and computer services for the whole department have been centralized in the planning division. The planning division is also responsible for coordinating the data basis of departmental policy with the short and medium range financial planning in the Ministry of Finance. Feeding back this information to the department's other divisions is also an important service function of the planning division. As will be seen, this mixture of directive and service functions is of special importance for the effectiveness of the division's work.

The planning division in the Ministry of Labor was established in 1968, growing out of a former staff unit. When a top level planning staff reaches a certain size, there seems to be a general tendency to incorporate it into the regular structure as subdivision or division. Until 1969, when a new division head took office and the statistical, mathematical, and computer services were integrated into the planning division, this planning unit lived in permanent conflict with the department's other divisions. This had a number of reasons. The section heads in the new division were partly recruited from outside of the department. They were economists by training and had therefore some difficulties to cummunicate with the other section heads with a training in law. More important still was the fact that the planning division started to engage in substantive planning and attempted to monopolize major policy developments within the department. This interfered heavily with the work of the other divisions which thereupon started to isolate the planning unit by withholding information from it. Moreover, while the unit was still located as a top level staff, it did not perform any service functions for the department, but was at the same time so closely identified with the departmental executive that the combined result was a distant and antagonistic relationship to the division.

The various reasons for the ensuing conflicts and the threatening ineffectiveness of the planning staff were recognized by the executive. After 1969 deliberate attempts were made to change the situation. The new divisional leadership did no longer attempt to monopolize the function of developing policy initiatives and planning major programs, but emphasized the division's coordinating and directive functions instead. At the same time the concentration of the department's statistical, mathematical, and computer services in the planning division prepared the ground for an essentially cooperative relationship with the other divisions. This cooperative relationship was strengthened by an incipient system of rotation of section heads between the divisions. Since the planning staff had become a division, not just a section or subdivision, the unit also retained its direct access to and close relationship with the departmental executive. The change in organizational location also made the situation easier for the departmental executive, which earlier was repeatedly confronted with the choice of either having to antagonize the divisions or to disavow its own staff.

Taking the case just described as an example, we can formulate the following preconditions for the effectiveness of a special planning unit which directs and coordinates the substantive planning activities of the department but does not engage in this work itself. Obviously such a unit must have a sufficiently large size. Insufficient size means that attention and direction must be so highly selective that the coordination function can no longer be performed. The interventions of a staff which is too small to perform its function properly can easily become a disturbance rather than helping with the department's work.

An important condition of effectiveness is the relationship between the planning unit and the departmental executive. On the one hand the unit needs sufficient executive support to perform its directive function vis-à-vis the other divisions. But executive support alone is not sufficient. The unit rather needs an independent basis of power or influence so as not to be forced to call upon the authority of the departmental executive whenever some other unit in the department attempts to resist its directive or coordinative interventions. To be effective the unit must actually *increase* the executive's directive capacity by serving as an amplifier and transmission belt of its intentions, but it should not absorb too much executive attention itself in the process. In the example discussed above, this independent basis of power or influence was supplied by the regular division's dependence on the planning division's service capacity. Another important possibility is that the planning unit's leadership enjoys the support of important external groups, such as the majority party, the unions, etc. The divisional leadership then has an avenue of access to the political communication system which is independent of the minister and the state secretaries. Enjoying political support in their own right, the planning unit's leader will be sought out by the regular divisional leadership as potential promotors with whom one can talk over and clarify the chances and risks of a policy initiative without having to call upon the departmental executive. This means a genuine increase in the departmental organization's directive capacity.

Another important condition of effectiveness is a cooperative rather than antagonistic relationship with the divisions. The probability of resistance grows with the frequency and intensity of the planning unit's interference in divisional affairs. The divisions consider it an interference if the planning unit takes away their former responsibilities in the area of policy initiation and program development, imposes policy goals upon them, gives them orders concerning the details of program elaboration, or interposes itself in their formerly direct communication with the departmental executive. This means that other things being equal, a planning unit which restricts its activities to directing and coordinating the work of the divisions will meet with less resistance than one which attempts to monopolize the work of substantive planning in the department. Nevertheless, even the former type of unit can hardly avoid doing some of the things mentioned above some of the time. It is therefore important for it to preserve the divisions' good-will by offering them services or other help in exchange for their tolerance of its directive interventions.

If the planning unit does not succeed here, it will soon be confronted with a grave information problem. To be able to perform its directive functions (and even more so any functions of substantive planning), the planning unit must be extensively and intensively informed by the divisions about their relevant activities. This can be ensured only within limits by procedures formally instituted to this effect. The reporting system practiced in the Ministry of Labor, where all ideas for a new policy initiative had to be presented to the executive in the form of a brief statement before the first draft of a proposal could be worked out, also served as a source of information to the planning division. A specific directive to inform the planning division of all policy initiatives would not have had the same effect.

More important than formal procedures are often virtual constraints which motivate the divisions to inform the planning unit or which produce such information as an unavoidable byproduct. In the Ministry of Labor such a constraint was provided by the planning division's service capacity: if a division asked for specific data or computations, it had to inform the planning division incidentally about the project it was working on. Besides, the divisions knew that the planning division would later have to evaluate their proposals with respect to their financial and economic consequences and to harmonize them with the strictures of the budget. This motivated the regular divisions to inform the planning division rather early of their projects in order to avoid investing much time in fruitless ventures. It should be recognized, however, that these constraints worked so well in this case partly because the department dealt with rather clearly defined problems characterized by structured alternatives and a highly formalized, quantitative data basis. The difficulty of the planning unit's information problem is obviously in part a function of the nature of the task.

1.3 Centralized planning units

The difficulty of finding the time for long-range planning under the constant pressure of day-to-day activities and the special information needs of planning are reasons frequently cited to justify the creation of a new unit for the task of substantive planning. This holds for administrative organizations as it does for industrial firms. However, it obviously depends on the nature of an organization's task structure whether centralization of planning is meaningful. It may be feasible to concentrate program development in one special unit if most of an organization's activities consist in program implementation. But where, as in the federal bureaucracy, program development is a major part of the operative units' normal work, to isolate it from the rest of the sections' tasks and concentrate it in a central planning unit must appear a problematical solution already at first sight.

If program development accounts for a substantial part of the operative units' activities, the central planning unit would have to be very large, and its internal differentiation would probably have to replicate the division of labor between operative units in the department. Secondly, and closely related to the first point, the centralization of all substantive planning requires that the members of the planning unit do not only have the special competence of the planner (i.e. knowledge of planning techniques, large overview of the problem area), but that they also are intimately familiar with the details of the subject matter of every program to be developed by them. With the growing amount and heterogeneity of program developments in a department this is increasingly difficult to fulfill.

The main problem, however, concerns the relationship between the centralized planning unit and the regular divisions. The centralization of all program developments in one special unit would interfere strongly with the traditional distribution of responsibilities. The regular sections and divisions will resent and resist this, which would make the job of the planning unit a highly difficult one from the beginning. Since the conflict would necessarily be intense, it would this time not even solve the problem if the planning unit were able to offer services to the regular divisions. The planning unit could not rely on being sufficiently informed by the regular divisions and would therefore be forced to build up its own information-gathering system. Even if the centralized planning unit could succeed in this way to emancipate itself from the dependence on the data basis of the regular divisions, this would only mean that the latter are cut off from the whole process of policy-making, which would unavoidably lead to their demoralization.

It is not surprising, therefore, that there exists in fact no federal department where program development has been completely concentrated in one special planning unit. However, centralization of planning need not necessarily mean such concentration. Conceivably the process of program development could be structured hierarchically, with the central planning unit setting up a global frame of reference, or global plan, which the sections would elaborate, specify, and concretize. The distinction to the previously discussed type of planning unit with coordinating and directing functions may not seem very pronounced, but the difference is that in a hierarchized planning process the central unit does engage in substantive planning.

An example for what we have in mind can be found in the Ministry of Transport, where in one of the divisions a planning subdivision was created in order to develop an integrated traffic ways program, including airways, waterways, roads, and railways. Within the department there exists a regular division or subdivision for each of these policy areas. There was no intention to shift the responsibility for policy initiation and program development completely from the existing regular divisions to the new planning

115

subdivision. The longrange, integrated traffic ways program to be developed by the latter, was, however, expected to provide a framework within which the detailed work of the regular divisions should take place. This meant that sectoral planning had to take account of the interdependencies with other types and ways of traffic and transportation.

In spite of its restricted assignment the planning subdivision found it difficult to fulfill its task effectively. The longrange nature of the integrated traffic ways program and the unit's location as a subdivision made it difficult for it to receive sufficient executive attention and support. The planning subdivision's relationship to the regular divisions was fraught with conflict. The planning subdivision could not convince the regular divisions of the need to adapt their programs to a long-range integrated plan. It also did not successfully solve the problem of getting the relevant information from the regular departments. The planning subdivision did not only lack sufficient executive support, it neither had an independent power basis nor anything to offer the regular divisions in return for their compliance. In order to solve this grave information problem the planning subdivision instituted a joint planning committee and several work groups, composed of members of the regular divisions together with members of the planning subdivision. This improved the situation, and by the end of 1973 the traffic ways program had been submitted to and approved of by the cabinet.

While not without problems, this variant of centralization in planning does hold a certain promise. One other possibility is the temporary institution of special planning units for the generation of a particular program. In this form, centralization of planning can be found in some project groups, a type of unit discussed above in chapter V, 2.3.

2. Government-wide planning institutions [3]

There are differences between departments in the extent to which they have introduced procedural and structural innovations with the intention of improving their planning capacity, but on the whole these changes have not had the effect of basically changing the decentralized pattern of departmental policy-making with its noted shortcomings in the area of executive control. However, the departments did become more active in the field of policy-making

116

as a result of these reforms. This has in turn increased the need for top level coordination, control, and direction through government-wide planning institutions — unless federal policy-making is to disintegrate into a more or less incoherent set of departmental policies.

In the early years of the Federal Republic, the strong personality of Konrad Adenauer had made for a high degree of centralization in political decision-making. Adenauer had also used the Chancellor's Office as an instrument to facilitate his influence upon departmental policies. But beginning in 1962, when Adenauer was forced to accept a limit on his time in office, a process of decentralization of governmental decision-making to the departments set in. This trend was reversed only when the decline of economic growth rates and the resulting fiscal crisis made it clear that the unbridled growth of public expenditures had to be checked. Thus the first elements of political planning were introduced between 1966 and 1969 in the time of the Grand Coalition.

Since economic and financial problems motivated these attempts, the first instruments to be developed were those of financial planning, including in particular middle-range economic projections and middle-range financial planning spanning a period of five years. Along with these instruments, a network of bodies with advisory, information processing, and coordinating functions developed. This financial planning system has since been elaborated and improved, but not basically changed. [4]

Early hopes that the new financial planning would also serve as effective instrument for the central coordination and direction of departmental policy-making were soon disappointed. It became clear that the directive function of financial planning depends on the extent to which it is integrated with governmental policy planning. The latter, however, needed first to be developed. This task devolved upon the Chancellor's Office.

Traditionally the divisional organization of the Chancellor's Office attempts to replicate the existing division of labor between departments, with one unit in the Chancellor's Office covering the areas of responsibility of one or more ministries. During Adenauer's chancellorship a system of personnel rotation between the departments and the Chancellor's Office had existed. During the last years an effort was made to revive this system to facilitate gaining access to the informal communications networks of the departments. At any rate, the Chancellor's Office is usually quite well informed about policy projects of the ministries and can act as promotor of departmental programs at the cabinet level and in the legislature. But in its traditional form it was hardly able to develop an independent policy perspective. In order to stimulate government-wide policy planning a special planning staff was therefore established in the Chancellor's Office in 1967. However, this staff remained largely ineffective because it quickly ran into difficulties such as we discussed above in section 1.2: the staff's capacity was not adequate to its task and it was further restricted by the lack of cooperation from the line organization and by insufficient top level support.

These conditions changed when the Social-Liberal coalition was established in 1969 and Horst Ehmke came to head the Chancellor's Office as a minister. In 1970 he transformed the planning staff into a sizeable planning division headed by Reimut Jochimsen, a professor of economics newly recruited from the outside. Under his direction the planners were to provide better policy coordination, to aid the cabinet in setting government-wide policy priorities, and to generate substantive inputs into policy processes under a long-range perspective. [5]

The planning division immediately started to set up a computer-based information system to monitor departmental policy projects before they would reach the cabinet level. To this end a standard system for reporting departmental projects already in their initiation phase was devised. The system was to be managed and controlled by the newly appointed departmental planning commissioners. Despite unavoidable technical flaws in the beginning, this information system has improved early horizontal coordination among the departments, and it has also facilitated the planning of cabinet and parliamentary agendas. On the other hand, the reporting activities required by the system have always been burdensome for the departments and have contributed to their general skepticism toward the work of the planning division.

Skepticism turned into hostility when the planning division used the new information system to compile a "short list" of reform programs that should be given top priority for the remainder of the legislative period and submitted it to the cabinet without prior consultation with the departmental planning commissioners. This brought the departments up in arms against the Chancellor's Office, and ever since they have put up resistance against further steps toward government-wide policy planning by the Chancellor's Office.

118

Also in 1970 the planning division started to set up a number of project groups to develop a comprehensive, long-range policy perspective which might provide substantive inputs for policy-making. But the departments who were asked to delegate members to these project groups cooperated only reluctantly, and the task itself soon proved more difficult than expected. Eventually a joint federal-state venture in "comprehensive problem analysis" operating at a reduced level of aspiration evolved from this effort. The usefulness of these analyses is still questioned by the federal ministries. As of this writing, joint problem analyses have not yet been resumed following the 1972 election.

The disillusionment with the actual results of the attempts to establish government-wide policy planning and the intra-governmental conflicts provoked in the process led to a face-about in policy when the second Social-Liberal government took office in 1972. Minister Ehmke left the Chancellor's Office and was replaced not by another minister but by a permanent secretary. Soon afterwards the head of the planning division also left to become state secretary in the Ministry of Education. The Chancellor's Office de-emphasizes again its political and programmatic functions, restricting its substantive influence upon departmental policies mainly to those areas which the chancellor himself and his political aides are able to influence through their personal involvement.

Chapter VIII

CONDITIONS OF ACTIVE POLICY-MAKING IN THE FEDERAL BUREAUCRACY

After an extended discussion of the macro-structure of the federal action system, of the personnel resources available to the government, of the internal organization of federal departments, of their policy-making processes and emergent planning systems, we now return to our more basic concern with the prerequisites of active policy-making. In our earlier discussion, we have focussed primarily upon the external conditions affecting the availability of financial, informational, organizational and political resources. After having identified and described the ministerial organization as the major actor within the federal action system, we will now focus upon the internal conditions affecting its ability to utilize available resources for active policy purposes.

1. Resource management

The scarcity of financial resources is a condition that policy-making in the Federal Republic will have to live with during the years ahead. So are the rapidly increasing demands of high-priority policy goals upon the resources available to government. And there is also no reason to assume that the goal conflict between the dual functions of government revenue and expenditure decisions as instruments for financing substantive policy programs and as instruments of anti-cyclical fiscal policy will disappear within the near future. Under such conditions, the quality of resource management within the government must be regarded as the one critical variable that may make the difference between an increasingly unmanageable 'fiscal crisis of the state' [1] and some more successful modalities of crisis management. At a very general level, the relative success or failure of resource management will depend upon the degree to which the government is able (a) to allocate scarce resources to priority policy areas; (b) to design and implement effective programs within these areas; and (c) to assure the efficiency of resource utilization within these programs. Before an evaluation of existing practices of financial management under these criteria can be attempted, the federal budgetary process must be at least briefly described.

1.1 The budgetary process

Its central instrument is still the annual budget proposed by the cabinet and enacted by the legislature in the form of a statute. Since 1967, however, the budget is supplemented by a middle-range financial plan for a five-year period of which the first year coincides with the current budgetary year. It is a 'rolling plan' in the sense that it is annually extended one year into the future and, at the same time, revised *in toto* on the basis of the most recent data and projections. Procedurally, it is significant that the budget and the financial plan are developed in one and the same decision-making process within the government, but that the financial plan is only adopted and published by the government, rather than enacted by the legislature.

The budgetary cycle for the year after next generally begins in November or early December with the budget letter of the Minister of Finance, containing guidelines for the revision of the financial plan and for the next budget based upon middle-range projections of economic development, recent tax estimates and, for the budget, upon departmental ceilings contained in the last financial plan. From then on, the departments have about three months in which to work out their draft budget and their estimates for the financial plan. Within the departments, the process begins in the individual sections whose requests are aggregated and, sometimes, reduced by the division heads before they reach the budget section within division Z. Here, the total requests have to be worked over in order to bring the department's proposal more nearly in line with the guidelines of the Ministry of Finance or, at least, with a somewhat realistic budget strategy of the department. In this process, the head of the budget section and the head of division Z

122

determine departmental policy on most individual points in bilateral negotiations with the individual divisions. The leadership will concern itself mainly with the sum total of the department's request, with major spending blocks and with some politically important budgetary items, but it will not, as a rule, attempt to undertake a systematic review of all items.

In February or March, the departmental requests and estimates are transmitted to the budget division in the Ministry of Finance which is almost as large as the Chancellor's Office. It is internally organized in four subdivisions, with the individual sections assigned to individual ministries. The budget division with its high prestige and its low personnel turnover has been able to accumulate a great deal of expertise regarding the programs and problems of individual ministries. But even with long memories and a highly developed ability to spot inflated claims, the budget officers must resort to some simple strategies in their unending struggle to bring demands in line with available resources. Experience has taught them that neither pre-determined departmental ceilings nor across-the-board percentage cuts will protect them against the skillful manipulation of political pressure to push through high-priority programs over and above general budget limitations. Only by looking closely at the individual spending items can they hope to identify budget cuts that will not be politically upset at the cabinet or parliamentary level. In this, they necessarily have to rely on rules of thumb which emphasize the close investigation of personnel increases, of new spending programs, and of programs rising faster than the average. These new and rising programs will be hit hardest by the need to economize while established spending items will pass through almost without a question.

Items on which agreement cannot be reached in bilateral negotiations at the section level will be pushed up progressively to the division heads, the state secretaries and, ultimately, to the ministers. In all these negotiations, two things are clearly understood by both parties: the Ministry of Finance will be responsible for presenting the budget proposal to the cabinet and, while any minister may place remaining points of disagreement on the cabinet agenda, this agenda will be very quickly overcrowded and, if it should come to a vote, the finance minister can be outvoted only by a majority of the cabinet that includes the chancellor. These are high obstacles, and the general result is that the Finance Ministry, (as long as the political reputation if its minister is intact) will have its way in most disputes before they reach the cabinet.

The cabinet usually votes on the draft budget and on the financial plan in July on the basis of the most recent economic projections, tax estimates, the recommendations of the federal-state finance-planning council. But the draft is submitted to parliament only in October or November. The time in between is used by the Finance Ministry and the departments in order to work out the fine details of departmental budgets within the framework determined by the cabinet. In a way, this amounts to a two-stage drafting procedure, in which the first stage can be characterized as a process of antagonistic bargaining over the maximum share that the department will be allowed, while the second phase should be seen more as a collaborative effort to eliminate imbalances and inconsistencies within a departmental budget after the question of total amounts has been settled. This two-stage procedure is a fairly recent and apparently useful innovation in the federal budgetary process.

At the parliamentary level, quite similar negotiations take place in the budget committee, with committee reporters for a particular ministry (one each from the government coalition and from the opposition) now assuming the role of the budget critic in search of opportunities to cut expenditures, while the budget division of the Finance Ministry and the departments will now jointly defend the government proposal. Budget changes in the parliamentary phase are by no means infrequent, but they also tend to focus upon unusual expenditure increases, thus reinforcing the tendency towards incremental budgeting that is inherent in the German as well as in the American budgetary process. [2]

By the time parliament comes to its final vote on the budget, it is usually April or May of the year to which the budget applies. Such delay is accepted as one of the inevitable facts of political life, and the constitution permits the finance minister to authorize necessary expenditures in the interim period. He utilizes this authority as one more instrument of his control over expenditure processes. The departments, which are allocated monthly instalments of their budget by the finance minister, have to operate under a restricted schedule during the first months of the year which makes budget surpluses (that cannot be transferred into the next year) more likely during the second half of the year.

The federal budgeting process as a whole seems designed to permit expenditure reductions at a great many stages in a process

124

in which the Ministry of Finance enjoys multiple opportunities for intervention and control. Thus it is, perhaps, understandable that not much political interest is generated by the ensuing auditing cycle in which the Federal Accounting Office reviews the legality of actual expenditures for each budgetary year in a report that is submitted to parliament and finally disposed of in a plenary vote exonerating the government from fiscal responsibility. Perhaps it is sufficient to characterize the relevance of the auditing phase by the fact that the final parliamentary vote may occur as late as six years after the budget year to which if refers.

1.2 Allocative efficiency

After this overview of the budgetary process we shall now return to our initial questions regarding the relative effectiveness and efficiency of resource management as a prerequisite of active policy making. Beginning with the question of allocative efficiency, it should have become obvious that the budgetary process with its decentralized, bottom-up spending initiatives and the incrementalist tendencies of budget review at the higher levels, is very poorly designed for the government-wide comparison of spending priorities. This general tendency is reinforced by two structural features: first, the budget as it is negotiated with the Ministry of Finance, adopted by the cabinet, and legalized by parliament, is the classical line-item budget, specifying expenditures by institutional units and by expenditure categories such as personnel, travel expenses, building maintenance, office equipment, postage and telephone expenses, and the like. Program categories are hardly visible in the budget proper. And while there is now a cross-reference system between line-item expenditures and functional spending categories that conform more closely to policy-relevant aggregates, the functional categories are included for informational purposes only and are not made the basis of actual budgetary decisions. All participants in the process, seem to feel much more comfortable and much more in control of what is going on, if they discuss budgets in terms of additional personnel positions or new office equipment or physical investments. These are concrete items, and these items are comparable across the divisions and across the ministries. They are, in a way, the common language of the budgetary process, while each of the separate policy areas would require its own language if it were discussed primarily in programmatic terms. As a consequence major spending blocks that cannot be disaggregated into small, familiar items, are often appropriated with very little critical review.

Perhaps even more detrimental to allocative efficiency is the fact that the main actors in the budgetary process apart from the spending divisions themselves are the specialized sections of the budget division and the equally specialized reporters of the parliamentary budget committee. They tend to become experts on the affairs of one ministry or even of a part of one ministry and they tend to develop the ability of judging the plausibility of budgetary claims within that area; but they are in no positions spending priorities across ministries. As the higher ranks in the Finance Ministry are without staff support, they are also unable to undertake an independent, comparative evaluation of departmental claims. They will, at least, develop a sensitivity to the political respectability and urgency of individual claims as negotiations move up the hierarchy toward the ministerial and cabinet levels. Nowhere in the system is there a systematic, comparative evaluation of spending programs, and nowhere is there any comparative evaluation that would include ongoing programs as well as new, or increased spending requests. There is no assurance that the budget should reflect any rationally determined priorities of the government as a whole.

If this were all there is to allocative efficiency, the picture would be bleak indeed. If we are not wholly pessimistic, it is because of the role which middle-range financial planning has by now assumed in the budgetary process. Even though the financial plans are not legally binding in any way, they do shape the perspectives of all participants and they do provide important guide posts for the annual budget which all participants have come to accept at least as the legitimate starting point for further bargaining processes. [3]

Two aspects help to make the financial plan a more useful instrument for setting policy priorities than the annual budget. The first is its wider time horizon which reduces the share of predetermined commitments and increases the maneuvering space in which changes in allocation are at all possible. Secondly, the financial plan is not drawn up in the lineitem categories of the regular budget. Instead, it uses highly aggregated functional categories, often at the level of total ministerial budgets, or of major spending programs which are large enough and few enough to be discussed and compared at the top policy-making levels. Thus, the haphazard pattern of spending increments in the annual budgets is replaced by more deliberate political decisions determining differential rates of growth for major spending categories over the middle range.

1.3 Program effectiveness

So far, the rationalization effect of financial planning is restricted to macro-level allocations to very broad, highly aggregated spending categories. Financial planning has not yet been effectively linked with program planning except in a few isolated experiments with a PPB-like program structure in some departments. Perhaps, this is to be expected in view of the methodological, organizational, and political difficulties that PPB as an attempt to systematically combine program and budget planning in one integrated instrument has run into everywhere. [4] Furthermore, as was pointed out above, program planning itself is by no means established even for major programs in all departments, and it has never really taken hold at the government-wide level. Thus, existing planning systems cannot provide the assurance that funds allocated to major spending categories will in fact be spent for programs which are effective in achieving their goals.

If forward-looking planning systems do not seem to promise quick improvement in overall program effectiveness, perhaps more significant gains should be expected from the backward-looking review and evaluation of ongoing programs. Systematic policy evaluation might provide pertinent and reliable feedback information that could be used for decisions on the continuation or termination or on substantive and procedural changes in ongoing programs. As a matter of fact, policy review is much more frequent in the federal government than systematic policy planning. The government itself produces a host of reports on the state of the health system, the social security system, the education system, research, transportation, or agriculture, as well as annual economic and financial reports which are required by statute. Parliament also does create commissions of inquiry to investigate certain policy areas, and individual ministries have frequently commissioned studies of the effectiveness and the impact of their policies, of which some of the better known ones, carried out by commercial research institutions, have produced devastating critiques of the effectiveness of small business subsidies, of government support for the dairy industry, or of conditions in the construction industry. [5]

If despite considerable policy-reviewing activity its impact on policy must be considered slight, this seems to be primarily due to two reasons: First, if evaluative information should lead to the weeding out of ineffective programs it would need to be digested and utilized by central authorities in the individual departments, the Finance Ministry, or the Chancellor's Office. Thus, the lack of policy review staffs at the higher levels eliminates much of the potential impact which evaluation might have upon policy. Review information, if it is utilized at all, is utilized at lower levels and within the constraints of those sections and divisions responsible for the programs that are reviewed. They, of course, have no interest in abolishing ongoing programs on which their budgets, their staff size and their career opportunities depend. While they may be interested in improvements and, in particular, in expansions of their programs, basic reappraisals of existing policy patterns are unlikely to originate from the specialized units at the bottom of the ministerial hierarchy.

At these higher levels, another mechanism seems at work which tends to reduce the interest in reappraisal (and, therefore, in establishing adequate policy evaluation staffs): while an incoming government or a new minister may profit politically from a critical review of existing departmental policies, this motivation for change is strongest at the time when new men are still quite uncertain in their grasp of the situation. It tends to erode fairly rapidly when the new ministers are being educated by the bureaucracy in the intricacies of their job, the complexity of all problems and the relative wisdom of status-quo policies. At the same time, the longer ministers are on their job, the more they are politically identified with ongoing departmental policies. After a while, the government as a whole and each departmental minister will respond to critical evaluations with justifications, counterattacks, and a remarkable unwillingness to reconsider the substance of ongoing programs. In a political culture where competition operates on all levels of the political and bureaucratic system but where job rotation at the cabinet level is comparatively rare, a prevalence of self-justifying over self-critical reactions must be counted amongst the political facts of life. As a consequence, policy evaluation can hardly realize its potential usefulness outside of the brief period after a change in government, unless strong external pressure, or the compulsion of an acute fiscal crisis, help to overcome the self-stabilizing tendencies of existing policy patterns.

We have considered resource management first under the aspect of allocating funds to policy priorities, then under the aspect of selecting effective programs (and eliminating ineffective programs) within policy areas. If significant breakthroughs toward a more rational system of resource management seem hard to achieve on these two fronts the efficiency of resource utilization within new or ongoing programs could still be a major factor affecting the overall degree of financial scarcity which constrains active policy making. Yet, it is at this level of resource utilization that the German fiscal system seems most problematical. One major factor is the rapid growth and the extreme inflexibility of the public service personnel system which gives rise to the suspicion that the rise of personnel costs might not be associated with similarly rising service levels. Still, given the distribution of adminsitrative functions, personnel costs affect the federal government somewhat less than state and local governments.

Another cause, which operates on all levels of government, can be found in the prevailing practices of budgetary management. Analytically, the efficiency of resource utilization can be defined in terms of the opportunity costs of expenditures. Searching for the most efficient mode of resource utilization makes sense only if the resources saved in the implementation of one program can be used for other purposes. While such opportunities do, of course, exist for the government as a whole and for the Finance Ministry, they are not necessarily relevant for the specialized, lower-level units whose requests stand at the beginning of the budgetary cycle and who will actually spend the allocated funds. Specialized units will tend to disregard opportunities outside their own area of responsibility — they tend to be 'budget maximizers'. [6] Therefore the more central participants in the budgetary process tend to look at the spending behavior of lower-level units with distrust. They react with closer scrutiny of budgetary requests, with an attempt to specify in great detail the permissible uses of funds and with close supervision of the actual use of allocations for these specified purposes. Such a practice reduces, and is intended to reduce, the discretion of lower-level units in the use of their budgeted funds. But, unfortunately, it also reduces their remaining motives to spend funds efficiently for their own programs. As long as funds saved cannot be used for other expenditures and cannot be transferred to the next year, the lower level units have in fact every reason to spend all their allocations as specified, regardless of obvious opportunities for more efficient uses. It is a self-reinforcing cycle in which fiscal centralization reduces opportunity costs for the lower level units which, with no reason to consider alternative uses, will tend to spend as much as they can get away with, thus justifying still greater fiscal centralization.

Fiscal centralization might be quite acceptable, if the resulting detailed appropriations were likely to approximate our optimal pattern. Unfortunately, they tend to be poorly informed and suboptimal from a program perspective. For even if exceptionally qualified, the budget officers in the ministries and in the budget division of the Ministry of Finance cannot become experts on the substantive aspect of the dozens of different programs whose budgets they have to review and control. Distrustful of the self-serving claims of the specialist units, and unable to absorb and interpret much relevant program-specific information, they must inevitably apply simple rules-of-thumb. But as long as budget details are determined by budget officers who must disregard most of the information that is specific to a particular program, it is almost inevitable that detailed allocations will be suboptimal. Unfortunately, such misallocations are not self-correcting when lower-level units (where program-specific information is available) are not free to reallocate funds within their own budgets. There are some indications, however, that the two-level budgetary procedure described above, in which a second round of negotiations with the Finance Ministry takes place after the cabinet has fixed the ceilings for the major budget categories, is being used for a more optimal fine-tuning of allocations. Freed from the pressure of having to balance total requests with available funds, and from the behavior patterns of antagonistic bargaining, the budget officers will listen more attentively to program specific arguments. And without the opportunity to increase their overall budget ceiling, program officers will be able to present their real priorities in a more straight forward fashion that helps to reduce somewhat the inefficiencies of budgetary centralization.

But this is modest progress, at best. Major breakthroughs in budget efficiency would probably depend upon the introduction of some variant of program budgeting which would focus the attention of the more central participants in the budgetary process upon the allocation of funds to specified program categories, leaving the micro-allocation of resources within these categories more to the lower-level units responsible for developing and implementing the programs themselves. Very cautious moves in that direction in the Ministry of Agriculture seem to have met with less resistance from the Ministry of Finance than one might have expected. But it is still much too early to judge the success of this experiment.

2. Information gathering and processing

The political systems's information gathering and processing capacity influences the effectiveness of policy decisions, in so far as this depends on the correctness of the factual premises on which the decisions are based. Moreover, since to control the information premises of a decision means to influence substantively its content, the ability of the federal bureaucracy to control the sources, the selection, and the utilization of information is also an important condition of the political system's autonomy. Decision quality and political autonomy are therefore the two relevant consequences of the federal bureaucracy's information system in the context of the present discussion.

In chapter II we pointed out that a policy which aims to direct complex and highly interdependent socio-economic processes has to meet specific informational requirements, both in terms of scientific knowledge and in terms of data which describe the relevant characteristics of the environment. Of course, successful policy decisions also require what may be called strategic knowledge concerning the goals and action tendencies of the various actors in the political system. But while statistical data and scientific knowledge are mainly required and utilized by the basic operating units of the federal bureaucracy engaged in developing programs of active policy, "strategic" information (which largely consists of singular descriptive statements) is typically sought by the political leadership and is not specific to active policy-making. In this section we shall concentrate on the scientific and statistical information needed by the federal bureaucracy.

The crucial importance of the federal bureaucracy's information system derives not only from the fact that the federal ministries are the most important policy makers (and hence information users) within the political action system at the federal level, but the federal bureaucracy also controls, collects, and processes most of the information relevant to policy decisions. The Ministry of

Science [7] is responsible for developing governmental science policy. The Federal Statistical Office and the information collected by the individual ministries are the most important sources of statistical information also for the parliamentary groups of the parties and for the government. Finally, it is the ministries and not parliament or the political parties to which organized interests turn first, where they argue their demands in detail, and to whom they present information in support of their claims.

2.1 Information supply and demand

In chapter II we discussed certain external conditions which limit the available information, especially of the scientific type. The general availability of information that would be needed for an active policy is of course not simply a given external restriction, but is intimately linked with the political system's own behavior. It depends on the information gathering capacity of the political system how much of the obtainable information is in fact collected, while the longterm growth of scientific information may be influenced through an effective science policy.

The potency of the information gathering system is, however, only one condition for achieving a satisfactory level of information. It is not only useless but a waste of time and money to collect more information than can be processed. The capacity for information processing is therefore a second condition of importance; it restricts the potentially positive effect of additional information on the quality of decision-making. The actual utilization of information in decision-making depends finally on a third factor, whose crucial importance is often neglected. This factor is the articulated, or active, demand for information.

In a recent study Witte has challenged on empirical grounds the tacit assumption of many information system builders that decision-makers know what information they need, and express this as information demand. [8] The demand for a specific piece of information presupposes that its relevance to the problem is recognized, which becomes more difficult as the problem gets more complex and is more unique in character. In addition to this cognitive factor, the articulation of a specific information demand is also inhibited by the expectation that the needed information is not available, by the realization of one's own limited processing capacity, and by attitudinal factors. In the federal bureaucracy as in other organizations the combined result of the operation of these factors is a more or less pronounced depression of information demand, so that the search for information probably stops well below the optimal level. Most important among the factors reducing information demand in the federal bureaucracy is probably the time pressure under which the administrative decision-makers operate. They must meet deadlines with their program drafts, and since the work capacity of the sections which do most of the actual drafting is very limited, there is a strong pressure to restrict the time spent in searching for information and the amount of information to be processed.

The limited use made especially of scientific knowledge in policy-making is therefore only partly due to the lack or the poor quality of available information. Where no demand is felt for a particular information, it will not be used even if it is being offered. Thus natural as well as social sciences have repeatedly signalized and analyzed emerging problems, e.g. in the areas of environmental deterioration, resource depletion, old age, education, or urban development, but were not heeded until acute pressures or a manifest crisis impelled political decision-makers to listen. The reactive nature of policy-making is itself one of the reasons which restrict the utilization of available information.

Due to the reactive nature of much policy-making, information demand also arises often quite suddenly as a problem becomes acute. If in such cases the needed information is not available but requires original data-collection or even scientific research, a radical discrepancy develops between the time requirements of these search processes and the short time-span available for finding a political solution. Typically, the major lines of the new policy are decided upon before the information specially collected as a basis for these decisions has become available. This has happened in the Federal Republic for instance in developing recent program of educational reform, of university reform, of administrative reform, and of regional development (*Raumordnung*).

2.2 The collection and sources of information

The federal bureaucracy makes use of several sources for the information it needs. Descriptive data and statistical information are to a large extent collected by public administration itself. Scientific information is mainly received from scientists and the institutions of science. Both data and scientific information are to some extent also supplied by interest organizations, who at the same time make the goals and action tendencies of relevant client groups known to the bureaucracy. We shall consider these various information sources in turn.

Agencies which implement the programs developed in the federal ministries are an important source of information which is descriptive of current situations. But the federal ministries have not always easy access to this information source. Where a ministry has close ties to the agencies which implement its programs, such as is true for the Ministry of Labor and the Federal Labor Agency, or the Ministry of Transport and the Federal Railroad, the information feedback follows institutionalized channels of upward communication. But where the programs a ministry develops are implemented by state and local agencies, the federal structure proves a barrier to the information feedback from the sites of program implementation. [9] This problem is felt acutely in ministries which have neither dependent agencies nor lower administrative extensions for implementing their programs and which are therefore neither in the position to prescribe the information to be collected by the field offices nor to demand being regularly informed by them.

The feedback from implementing agencies can take various forms, from sporadic and unsystematic qualitative accounts of problems encountered to elaborate statistics about the cases dealt with etc. Statistical information is also collected by various offices established expressly for this purpose, such as the Federal Statistical Office, government supported institutes which provide specialized statistical (especially economic) information such as the *Deutsche Institut für Wirtschaftsforschung*, and in part also specialized sections within individual departments. If we are to believe the federal bureaucrats involved in policy development, this system of data collection meets their informational requirements only insufficiently. Only few federal bureaucrats express satisfaction with the current standard of information. Their specific complaints refer first and foremost to the incompleteness or lack of statistical data that would be needed for program development, which is mainly attributed to a system of data collection insufficiently geared to the needs of policy-making. A second group of criticisms refer to information storage and distribution. It is said that finding a specific item of information is often too time-consuming, that data are often not aggregated or are not presented in the form in which this is needed, and that at other times one is flooded with too much useless information.

134

Even if it is difficult to assess the weight of these criticisms in objective terms, they probably do all point to real shortcomings. As far as the supply of statistical information is concerned, this may be due to several reasons. Most departments do not have the work capacity to engage in time-consuming procedures of original data collection. The Federal Statistical Office, on the other hand, enjoys a relatively high degree of autonomy. The departments can of course formulate their demands, but even where the Statistical Office is willing to include some additional statistics in its program, the data often arrive too late for the task for which they were needed.

Besides, there are considerable difficulties in adapting the traditional categories in which statistical data are collected, or in which implementing agencies report back to higher levels, to newly recognized informational needs. Information of the descriptive type may not supply innovative problem solutions, as scientific knowledge does, but it can identify the existence or incipient growth of problems, provided that the relevant aspects of the environment are being observed. Efforts to adapt and extend the information gathering system to this purpose are currently being made, as illustrated by attempts made in the Ministry of Labor to develop a system of social indicators. [10] These instruments, however, take more time to develop than it took to recognize the new information needs in general and abstract terms.

The major external sources of information for the federal bureaucracy, contact with organized interests and cooperation with science, have a common history and are even today frequently found in combination. In Germany, attempts to establish bodies which could provide expert advice on specific policy matters to the bureaucracy date back to the beginning of the 19th century. [11] More or less from the start these advisory bodies had a mixed character, serving both to provide expert advice and to institutionalize interest representation vis-à-vis public administration. These mixed commissions, which include interest representatives as well as independent experts among their members, are even today the most frequently found type of commission associated with the federal bureaucracy. They may provide some scientific information, but their main purpose is to articulate the demands and wishes of special groups, to provide the administration with situational information relevant to the development of specific programs, and to build up support for the policy being developed. In contrast, plainly scientific advisory commissions have been established only after 1945, and play a minor role among the plethora of commissions serving the federal bureaucracy. [12]

The groups affected by the policy developed in the federal ministries can argue their demands and their view of current policy proposals not only in the mixed commissions, but also in bilateral contacts with the bureaucracy. The Joint Manual of Procedure states that in the development of all major program proposals, the top interest organizations in the field may be heard, and this is usually done. [13] The consultation usually takes place between the section and/or division heads concerned and top functionaries of the interested organizations. These contacts are held to be very useful by the bureaucracy, and they fulfill mainly the same functions for it as do the mixed commissions mentioned above — maybe with the difference that the forum of a commission which also includes independent experts obliges the interest representatives to argue their point rather than to bargain and use pressure, which increases their value as an information source and provides for a built-in check of informational manipulation.

From the perspective of active policy-making, this pattern of consultation with organized interests has two problematical aspects. One is its selectivity. Because of their limited work capacity, the federal departments restrict their search for relevant situational information to contacts with the major organized interests. [14] This means that they can and do not systematically inquire into the situation and wishes of socioeconomic groups which are not organized and have a low potential of engaging in conflict with the administration, or of creating political difficulties. The information input from the relevant sectors of the administration's socio-economic environment is therefore selective in a way which restricts the chances for an active policy.

The second problem lies in a potential loss of autonomy if the departments, due to their limited work capacity, become dependent upon organized interests as a source of situational analysis and of policy proposals. The impression gained from a number of case-studies [15] indicates, however, that such an informational dependence is in most cases not an acute danger. Partly for reasons of their own limited work capacity and the lack of an appropriate apparatus, partly due to a predominantly defensive orientation, interest organizations rarely offer fullfledged program proposals or try to initiate policy. This may not hold for some potent organizations such as The Federation of Labor (*Deutscher Gewerkschaftsbund*), but most interest organizations tend to react to the initiatives or proposals of the political system with specific criticisms and proposals for modification rather than taking the initiative themselves.

The federal bureaucracy's informational dependence on external sources is undoubtedly more pronounced in its relationship with science than in its relationship with organized interests. Of course, as we pointed out before, the federal bureaucracy need not search in the environment for all the scientific knowledge it requires, since a certain level of information is already provided through the training of its members, who also attempt to follow individually the scientific development in their respective fields. But this stored knowledge is often not enough to provide answers to specific questions, so that scientific advisors are called in or research projects are initiated to obtain the necessary information.

The research which the federal ministries initiate, directly as well as through their dependent agencies and lower level extensions, is partly conducted in government institutes and partly as contract research in independent institutes. In quantitative terms, contract research placed with independent research institutions, including university institutes, is at least as important for policy-making as direct government research. The number of government and especially of federal research institutions is rather small: Hirsch counted only 32 of the latter in 1969/70. [16] In addition, however, a number of formally private institutions are de facto government supported. But government owned as well as government supported institutes do not only work to supply scientific information to the ministries and other administrative agencies; they also engage in basic and in applied research of less specific relevance to policy-making.

The relationship of the federal ministries to the research institutions which they support or which are directly dependent on them is beset by a difficult control problem. To maintain tight control over a research institute is difficult enough for such objective reasons as lack of professional competence and a limited work capacity. But the research institutes which depend on government support also strive actively for as much autonomy as they can get, not only because this is a general tendency in organizations, but also because where science is involved independence has a particular normative value. The normative pressure of the constitutionally guaranteed freedom of science is also felt by the federal bureaucrats, and makes them yield the more easily to strategies of autonomization pursued by government institutes. As a consequence, government financed institutes are often set up to be formally independent, or are at least headed by an executive board or directorate in which government representatives occupy only part of the seats.

This general situation often results in two different, but equally problematical consequences. irrelevance, or dependence. In the first case the institutes, in defining their research priorities and projects, come to neglect the informational needs of the ministries to which they report or on which they depend financially, and thus loose immediate relevance for policy-making. Conversely, in some specific areas policy development may become all too dependent on the specialized information supplied by particular government institutes, which may even come to attempt deliberately to influence policy. True, a relation of dependence develops rarely and only in scientific fields where there is little or no independent research going on, so that a particular institute or group of institutes comes to enjoy a virtual monopoly. This situation is aggravated where through its board or directorate, the institute is influenced by powerful non-governmental interests. Rare as they may be, in such cases the political system's autonomy is clearly impaired.

The main problem in the case of contract research is not control but communication. While the use of government institutes as a source of information does at least permit the gradual development of a satisfactory mode of communication between policy-oriented civil servants and scientists, this is usually not the case where research projects are placed as contract research. The resulting difficulties of communication seriously limit the fruitfulness of this form of gathering information. The problem results in part from too infrequent contacts between the civil servants and the scientists involved. It is not an exceptional case that no contact takes place between a ministry and the scientist or institute from signing the contract until the finished report or expertise is delivered. Under these circumstances the expertise may easily answer a question which has meanwhile become irrelevant because the problem has been redefined in the ministry, or the scientists may have redefined the question put to them and therefore miss the point.

But these communication problems have also a more general aspect, which can be mitigated but not definitely resolved by finding different forms of cooperation. Governmental contract research brings the three diverse systems of science, politics and

138

administration into contact, each of which pursues its own interest, is subject to its own norms, and has its own ways of thinking and procedures of work. Communication between these systems requires a process of translation or transposition which frequently does not function well. This becomes very evident in the opinions expressed by federal bureaucrats involved in contacts with scientists in an interview study conducted by Friedrich. The criticisms made by his respondents of the limited usefulness of scientific advice refer in one form or the other to the basically different orientation of scientific experts, who appear to be unwilling or unable to accept the definition of a problem as the bureaucracy sees it and who therefore often miss the point in their analyses and proposals, whether they remain too abstract in their arguments, neglect problems of practicability, or fail to take into account political realities. [17]

This communication problem decreases where a department turns repeatedly to the same scientists or scientific institute for advice. Here the relationship gradually assumes an advisory character, with the scientists becoming more and more partici-pants in the problem solving process. Such an active participation is generally institutionalized in the role of expert advisor and particularly in commissions of the scientific, but also of the mixed type.

Advisory commissions which serve the bureaucracy are general-ly attached to the division or even section which is formally responsible for the subject matter in question. This means that sections and division heads rather than the departmental executive are the main discussion partners for the commissions even where, as is sometimes the case, the minister formally heads a com-mission. This organizational location of the advisory commissions is important for the function attributed to them: they are obviously not intended to give political advice, or advice to politicians, as the term *Politikberatung* would have it, but they stand in a service relationship to senior civil servants. The attribution of a service function to scientific advice is also very plain in the answers of the civil servants interviewed by Friedrich, who mention in particular such instrumental functions as provid-ing factual information and analyzing problem situations and trends of development, but rarely grant scientific advice a role in the crucial tasks of making proposals for action or of defining policy goals. [18] Nor is this simply a misperception of civil servants who are eager to reserve for themselves the task of making

139

policy proposals; these views reflect the actual function of advisory commissions as expressed in their official assignments and their operation.

It is, however, not only informational functions which the advisory commissions in particular and scientific advice in general serve. In the study by Friedrich two thirds of his respondents referred explicitly to the political functions of getting scientific advice. The political function is again predominantly of an instrumental kind, i.e. an active political role in the sense of influencing policy decisions is only rarely attributed to scientists, while the most frequently mentioned political functions of scientific advice are to justify decisions which would have been made anyway, or have been made already; to help putting off demands one does not wish to fulfill and to neutralize in this way the pressure of organized interests; and to give political decisions the appearance of scientific objectivity. These political functions of scientific advice are fully intended and manifest, and experts or commission members are often selected, or questions phrased in such a way as to make sure that the desired effect is produced. [19]

In spite of the attribution of mainly instrumental functions to scientific advice, Friedrich's study has shown that the federal bureaucrats perceive the danger of a potential loss of autonomy through a growing dependence on scientific advice, sometimes even painting the spectre of expertocracy in which outside experts supply the problem definitions and prescribe the course of action to be taken. This fear seems ill-founded in view of the predominant experience of a rather limited influence and the successful instrumentalization of scientific advice. But there are in fact some areas of highly specialized (mostly: natural science) knowledge where the bureaucracy is no longer competent to evaluate critically the advice it receives and where for instance the scientific director of a certain research institute may be said to influence policy effectively through his "advice".

On the whole, however, the problem of relevance, i.e. of getting from science what is needed for policy-making, seems still more important than the potential threat to the autonomy of the political system. The relevance or salience of on-going scientific research for policy-making could in the long run be increased by a governmental research policy which seeks to establish tighter control over the development of science, but such a policy easily gets into conflict with the constitutionally guaranteed freedom of science.

140

Aside from the instrument of research policy, there are also organizational changes which could improve the usefulness of scientific advice for policy-making. The current advisory system is too traditional in form, too little adapted to its potential function for developing policy. This is true of the organization of government research institutes; organizational forms might be devised which would permit a more positive solution of the control problem noted above, for instance by using financial constraints to assure the choice of relevant research problems and by creating an institutional basis for the continuous translation process between science and politics.

This translation process, however, must operate in both directions. If the bureaucracy can define research programs unilaterally, there is the tendency that such programs reproduce the fragmentation of responsibilities which characterizes departmental organization, preventing the comprehensive analysis of all aspects of a problem because certain of its components lie outside the commissioning unit's area of formal competence. This tendency, for which many concrete instances could be cited, would probably become more pronounced with the intensification of government control over policy-relevant research.

One example which seems to disprove these fears is provided by the Commission for Economic and Social Change, which sponsors an extensive research program characterized by comprehensive problem definitions. The individual projects are publicly announced and research institutes compete for them. The only drawback is that the commission is not a typical example of research sponsored by the bureaucracy. Having been instituted by the government itself, the commission is a rather independent body and possesses no line authority, which means that the research results obtained by it are likely to have little impact on departmental policy-making.

Organizational changes which might improve the usefulness of scientific advice for policy-making are also possible with respect to the advisory commissions, which suffer from being too big, from being able to work only intermittently and thus slowly and not very concentratedly, and which are hindered by cumbersome procedures. A further point of weakness is the recruitment of experts, both as individual advisors and as commission members, where there is a tendency to recruit "big names" rather than younger scientists who have enough time and interest to devote to such a task. Finally the whole advisory system is characterized by a pronounced lack of coordination, which results in much parallel work, or doubling, and provides neither for the exchange of information between departments about the scientists and institutes employed, nor about the projects sponsored and the results obtained. But there is resistance against attempts to increase coordination systematically, which follows not only from the eager defense of departmental autonomy, but also from the fact that for each subunit "its" own commission, scientific advisors, and research funds are important assets in the competition for prestige, influence, and organizational standing.

The foregoing analysis indicates that the system of information collection is less effective than it could be if concerted efforts were made to that purpose. This, of course, is not saying much, because it is normal for practically all organizational functions that they could be improved if they were made the focus of special efforts — except that this is not possible for all of them at the same time. Attempts are in fact continuously being made to improve various aspects of the information collection system. Bigger reform efforts may be inhibited by the recognition of the costs and possible negative side-effects which the radical change of present patterns would involve, but also by the fact that with all its shortcomings, the present information supply does not lag so much behind conscious demand — which may in turn be related to the fact of a limited capacity for information processing.

2.3 Aspects of information processing

The internal organization of information processing within the federal bureaucracy is characterized by a high degree of decentralization. Neither the departmental nor even the divisional leadership instruct the sections in detail as to the kind and amount of information they are to collect and use in connection with a given assignment. To decide what information they need in developing a program and to collect it is generally considered the task of the sections. Only where the sections want to employ external experts or to engage a research institute in their search for information the divisional and in some cases even the departmental leadership want to be consulted, mainly for financial reasons.

If there is no central departmental direction and control of policy-relevant information processing, there do exist specialized units within the departments which can assist the sections. In some departments this does not amount to more than information storage in the traditional form of archives or documentation. But where use is increasingly made of massive amounts of statistical data, such as in the Ministries of Finance, of Economics, of Labor, and of Transport, specialized statistical and computer units have been established which serve a division or even the whole department.

The extent to which electronic data processing equipment is being used by the federal bureaucracy may be taken as an indicator of the development of a modern system of information processing. In this connection it may be significant that of the 686 computers installed in the Federal Republic's public administration in 1971, nearly one third were counted at the federal level, where it took over 8000 persons to operate and service them. [20]

As happened previously in industry, automatic data processing has been used in public administration first and foremost to substitute the routine handling of large numbers of similar case, a characterization which applies more to program implementation than to policy-making. Not surprisingly, therefore, the most highly automated functions in the federal bureaucracy are budgeting and accounting, [21] the calculation and payment of salaries and pensions, and tax collection. But computers also provide help where elaborate statistical or mathematical calculations are needed in policy-making and other minsterial tasks.

The establishment of data banks and integrated information systems as an aid to decision-making is a more recent development. There are plans for a system of data banks, parts of which are already in the process of construction. The federal data bank system is to include a statistical data bank at the Federal Statistical Office; a criminal information system put up jointly by the Federal Criminal Office and the corresponding state agencies; a political data bank built up at the Federal Press and Information Office, and a data bank for the area of social welfare policy developed by the Ministry of Labor and Social Affairs. The Ministry of Defense with its lower level administrative extensions and the Armed Services also make intensive use of electronic data processing. The federal government supports a central research and training institution in the field of electronic data processing, the Society for Mathematics and Data Processing (GMD). This institution conducts basic research, develops some specific applications, and serves as training institution for the personnel needed by the federal bureaucracy.

It is interesting that the introduction of automated data

processing has not provoked any significant changes in administrative structure. At the federal level the new computer and data processing units have normally the status of a section, rather than being directly subordinate to the departmental executive as a special staff. While state and local authorities are developing vertically integrated systems, there is a strong tendency at the federal level for each ministry to build up its own information storage and processing system. The advice and coordination which the Ministry of the Interior attempts to provide is often less welcome than the help of independent agencies such as the GMD.

In spite of the existence of specialized units providing information services, the sections must invest a considerable amount of time in searching for the information they need, rather than being able to select from a constant inflow of information being offered to them without special request. This is not necessarily a drawback if one considers that the relevance of a piece of information is recognized only on the background of a specific problem, and that the information parameters (e.g. scope, time reference, level of disaggregation or aggregation) will be more to specification where information is requested. More serious is the limited work capacity of the sections which unavoidably results in a tendency to make do with as little information as possible, and to prefer that information which can be had without investing much time in collecting and processing it. This militates also against the use of time-consuming techniques of information processing and decision-making, such as cost benefit analysis, PERT, computer simulation etc. Except for some specialized planning units these techniques are not systematically used in the development even of large-scale programs. Aside from a lack of work capacity, the inadequate training of civil servants for the tasks of planning also plays a role in this.

We may conclude that in the collection as well as in the processing of information relevant for policy-making, the capacity of the federal ministries does not meet the demands of developing more complex, large-scale, and long-range programs. The restricted information processing capacity at least slows down the process of program development, so that the anticipatory direction of socio-economic processes becomes difficult, if not inachievable at times. Attempts to solve this problem by delegating the processing of information to external agencies, whether this means interest organizations or scientific organizations, pose a threat to the autonomy of the political system and have been largely avoided until now.

144

3. Coordination

In Chapter V, we have described the highly decentralized character of policy-making processes within the federal bureaucracy which — in view of the specific requirements of active policy formation — tend to be associated with critical shortcomings:

Being limited in their jurisdiction and their available resources, the policy-making units will limit their scope of attention to problems within their own area of responsibility and to solutions which are within their undisputed area of competence. As a consequence, even research programs commissioned by a department are carefully defined to avoid the appearance of looking beyond one's own jurisdiction and of meddling with somebody else's business. And, of course, the action programs which are proposed are even more sensitive to such organizational constraints.

But, of course, in the real world problem interdependencies will not stop at the lines of jurisdictional demarcation within the bureaucracy. Housing and urban development do hang together with urban transportation; the use of antibiotica and insecticides in farming may have an effect on food quality, and the immigration of foreign labor has its effects beyond the labor market on urban housing and education systems. Each of these fields falls into a separate jurisdiction. But if bureaucratic policy makers tend to limit their attention to problems and solutions for which they are immediately responsible, and if they disregard the existing interdependencies with other problem areas, they may focus upon the symptoms rather than the effective causes of a problem and they may devise solutions that cannot be effective because they do not reach far enough. At the same time, however, these narrowly conceived policies may have very real side effects beyond their specified target areas which, again, tend to be disregarded by the selective perception of jurisdiction-bound policy makers. Under a normative perspective, therefore, the bureaucratic world with its necessary division into precisely defined jurisdictions ought to allow for the recombination of its fragmented parts in policy-making processes dealing with interrelated problems and requiring concerted solutions. This is the core of the coordination problem in active policy-making.

Policy coordination is a task to which the prevailing inter-ministerial and intra-ministerial matrix structure, which was described above, does not provide very effective solutions. Of course, the budget and the middle-range fiscal plan do provide coordination, but primarily under the aspect of the allocation of scarce resources or policy inputs, rather than under the aspect of interrelated policy outputs and their impacts in the real world. Even if the budgetary process were not so exclusively determined by a fiscal-resource perspective, the organizational specialization by departments in the budget division of the Finance Ministry would make effective inter-departmental coordination through the budget rather unlikely. Similarly, other effective matrix functions such as personnel, organization, or law also seem to be rather unsensitive to substantive policy interdependencies.

The situation is somewhat different with regard to the more output-oriented matrix functions such as foreign relations, development aid, environmental protection, or regional policy (*Raumordnung*), all of which have been institutionalized in specialized departments or divisions but are largely defined in terms of their influence upon the substantive policies of other departments. Here, the intention to coordinate policy can be assumed. But, unlike the Finance Ministry, these coordinators do not control essential inputs and do not dispose of effective functions vis-à-vis those departments whose activities they should coordinate. Thus, their influence will largely depend upon the voluntary cooperation of other departments.

If the matrix structure could provide, at best, a partial solution to the coordination problem, the alternative of central coordination appears even less effective in the federal bureaucracy. The chancellor, and the Chancellor's Office are not the hierarchical superiors of the ministries. And while the Office exercises some influence on departmental policy proposals through its management of the cabinet agenda and, of course, through its briefings of the chancellor, it cannot exploit this influence very aggressively without loosing the informal sources of information upon which its effectiveness depends. As was pointed out in Chapter VII, the attempt of the planning division in the Chancellor's Office to set up a central information and coordination system for departmental policies was largely abandoned after the elections of 1972, so that government-wide central policy coordination is presently not a live option. Similarly, the weakness of central policy staff in most ministries still restricts the scope of central policy coordination at the departmental level.

What remains is horizontal self-coordination among the divisions within a department and among the departments. It is sanc-

146

tioned at the departmental level through the need to obtain the approval of the minister for divisional proposals, and the common practice of all ministers to request the opinion of other interested divisions in the department before a final decision is reached. The same pattern is followed at the cabinet level where nothing is more damaging to a departmental initiative than the opposition of another department, with a legitimate interest in the proposal, that was not consulted before the proposal reached the cabinet. Thus, the federal bureaucracy has developed a high sensitivity to the interests of other units that ought to be consulted in policy-making processes, and in cases of doubt it is standard practice to opt for more, rather than less consultation. In most areas where frequent, multi-lateral contacts are required, consultation has become routinized in interministerial committees operating at the various levels of the bureaucracy all the way up to cabinet committees. [22]

But horizontal self-coordination may take quite different forms with widely differing substantive consequences. For analytical purposes, we will distinguish between two ideal types which we call 'negative coordination' and 'positive coordination' even though we realize that they describe extremes on a continuum rather than dichotomous alternatives. [23] Prevailing practice conforms most closely to the model of negative coordination: here, policy initiatives are restricted to the jurisdiction of one specialized section or division. Within this area, the initiating unit will analyze policy problems and propose policy solutions, very often without regard to their consequences for other areas. But other units, responsible for connected problem areas, will be consulted and they will examine the initiative strictly from the perspective of their own jurisdictions. If they have reason to expect infringements of their jurisdiction or negative repercussions upon areas under their responsibility, they will try to use consultation in order to eliminate these detrimental side effects of the initiative.

Given the limited capacity of the cabinet for conflict resolution and its preference for agreed-upon proposals, the opposition of another department may frustrate any proposal or, at least, cause unacceptable delay. As a consequence, initiating units will usually respond to powerful objections from other departments by offering adjustments. But such compromises will often reduce the scope of innovative policy proposals and the effectiveness of problem solutions surviving pre-cabinet bargaining processes. In this sense, negative coordination tends to work against the requirements of active policy-making.

147

While negative coordination is the prevailing practice in the federal bureaucracy, its alternative, positive coordination, is more easily defined than practiced. It would require the merging of the attention spaces and of the action potentials of units responsible for connected problem areas. Under such conditions, the interdependent problems could be subjected to inclusive analyses, and integrated policies could be designed which would permit a concerted attack upon the most effective causes within the problem configuration. To achieve this degree of integration of analysis and policy, the organizational division of labor would have to be temporally suspended.

Such attempts have been undertaken fairly frequently in recent years through the establishment of project groups to which we referred above in Chapter V, 2.3. With full-time or part-time staffs drawn from the membership of separate ministries or divisions supposedly involved in a common problem, such project groups are generally set up in the hope of obtaining integrated policy proposals based upon the combined perspectives of the participating units. On the whole, however, the success of project groups in the federal government has been less than spectacular, and the initial enthusiasm has given way to a good deal of skepticism during the last few years.

Such skepticism is not necessarily due to bureaucratic conservatism or to human inadequacies. There seem to be at least two factors working systematically against the success of integrated policy-making through groups dispensing with the organizational division of labor. The first reason is very straigthforward. The complexity of policy analysis and the resulting information load will increase exponentially with the number of separate information sets that need to be combined in analysis. Given the limited capacity of the human mind and the resulting need for informational specialization, any inter-divisional or inter-departmental project group will depend heavily upon the capacity of intersubjective communications and upon learning processes which will quickly break down when overloaded with heterogenous information. While the capacity of group information-processing may be increased, it is easy to overstep any conceivable limits when the area of analysis is expanded to include additional information sets. Unlike negative coordination, an inclusive solution requires every participant to evaluate every contribution not only with respect to his own area of responsibility but with a view to the desirability of the overall solution in terms of its impact upon all affected sectors. These requirements are so demanding that the conditions of positive coordination could, at best, be fulfilled for fairly narrowly defined problem clusters. If project groups should exceed the maximum capacity of group information-processing, they will end in the frustration of total confusion rather than in positive coordination. This is an experience which some of the project groups that were established at the federal level over the last few years have had to suffer.

Where projects groups do not have to capitulate before unmanageable complexity, they may be frustrated by unmanageable levels of conflict. This was certainly true of the joint planning groups of the federal government and the states in areas where either the economic interests or the ideological goals of the participants were sufficiently diverse to make voluntary consensus unlikely. This was so in joint federal-state planning in the areas of education and of regional development, and it also happens in interministerial project groups whenever there are serious conflicts of interest. If deadlock is not an acceptable solution for the promotors of new policies, they are forced to seek agreement on a level that is acceptable to a 'minimum winning coalition'. What is a winning coalition depends, of course, upon the decision rules which, in federal state negotiations, tend to require either unanimity or three-quarters-majorities in bodies in which the federal government has the same number of votes as the states. In both cases, the consent of opposition governed states is essential to any agreement on joint federal-state policies.

Obviously, neither the frustrations of over-complexity nor of unresolvable conflicts of interest or of ideology are very conductive to active policy-making. Thus, inter-ministerial project groups and federal-state joint planning groups have not been very successful instruments of positive coordination so far. If positive coordination is to be achieved at all, there is, first, a need for the deliberate management of complexity in which positive coordination should be treated as a scarce commodity that needs to be reserved for highly connected policy clusters. Analytical procedures for identifying such clusters of inter-dependent policy areas have been proposed, but they have not yet reached the operational level. [24]

At the same time, the problem of conflict resolution in coordination processes needs much more attention than it has received so far. Coordination may be a highly asymmetrical relationship in which power and, in particular, veto power may be of crucial importance. Coordinators without effective power may be easily frustrated. This seems to be true of coordination attempts by the ministries responsible for development aid, environmental protection and regional policy at the federal level. Similarly, in the relationship between the federal government and the states since 1969, when the institutionalization of joint planning systems did neutralize the instrument of federal grants-in-aid as an effective sanction applied by the federal government. [25] In the absence of hierarchical or financial sanctions, the outcome of inter-departmental or federal-state coordination seems to depend very much upon which of the participants may be capable of unilateral action. At the level of the federal government, this is more true of the spending departments than of the coordinating departments. And in the relationship between the federal government and the states, this is more true of the states with their plenary powers of administration than of the federal government which depends upon state administration. In both areas, the result is either non-coordination or agreement at the level of the least common denominator, neither of which create very favorable conditions for active, concerted policy-making.

4. Conflict resolution

In chapter II, where we dealt with support as a political resource, we pointed out that the ability to resolve conflicts and achieve consensus is a crucial prerequisite for active policy-making. We shall now discuss the role of the federal bureaucracy in this process, beginning with some remarks about the conflicts which arise within the federal bureaucracy itself.

4.1 Conflicts within the federal bureaucracy

Within the federal bureaucracy there occur both conflicts over policy content and conflicts over the distribution of formal competence, resources, and personal rewards. Both types of conflict are related to the fact of structural differentiation, i.e. the creation of sub-units with different tasks.

Conflicts over policy content can arise between the policymaker and the target group of his policy if the latter opposes the policy's goals and/or the measures proposed to reach them. Such conflicts occur rarely within the federal bureaucracy, except in cases like an

150

administrative reform program which involves the bureaucracy itself as a target group. Instead, these conflicts in the goal-dimension typically involve the bureaucracy with groups in the socio-economic environment, which, however, may find a sponsor in the bureaucracy who represents its interests and engages vicariously in conflict with other ministries.

Intra-organizational conflicts over policy content, on the other hand, occur mainly in the lateral dimension, involving off-target groups affected by a policy. These conflicts over policy are typically conflicts between different policies carried forward by different organizational sub-units who are trying to prevent negative repercussions on their own projects from the policy followed by another sub-unit. Such conflicts arise because the policies of different sub-units in the bureaucracy cannot be realized independently of each other; they may be incompatible or produce negative side-effects for each other. Where the sub-units involved identify in addition with the interests of different and conflicting socio-economic groups, the structurally determined conflicts are reinforced, because each client group will prevail upon "its" department or division not to make concessions in defending its interests against the encroachment of other policies.

There is yet a third kind of conflict over policy content which is neither a conflict between different policies nor a conflict of interest over policy goals, but derives from a difference of opinion over the best way to solve a problem and arises among those jointly responsible for formulating a given policy. Such differences of opinion can result from different professional perspectives, which may for instance set a legal expert and a professional chemist jointly concerned with formulating a piece of food and drug legislation against each other. This is of course a frequent kind of conflict within the federal bureaucracy, but since it is also a rather routine and every-day kind of conflict which is, moreover, not even always structurally determined and — by definition — not reinforced by conflicting outside interests, its intensity tends to be lower and its resolution easier than is the case with the previously discussed conflicts over policy content. This may not hold, however, for conflicts in the matrix structure, where professional and functional perspectives combine. These conflicts can become very bitter indeed.

Conflicts over formal competence for a given area of policy occur at all levels within the bureaucracy: between sections, between divisions, and between departments. Conflicts growing out of the competition for resources, on the other hand, are reduced by certain features of the federal bureaucracy. Within departments it is the pattern of stable resource allocation to the divisions and sections by means of the annual budget which reduces conflict, especially with respect to financial resources and personnel. Between departments conflict over resource distribution is reduced by the fact that each department recruits personnel and collects and processes information largely for itself; this also holds for technical and some other services. As for financial resources, the departments fight individually with the Ministry of Finance and not directly with each other; this indirect competition moreover takes place largely within the framework of the annual budgeting process, so that, when the annual allocations have been made, acute conflicts decrease.

The development of structurally determined conflicts in the federal bureaucracy is not only largely unavoidable, but in part even positively functional for policy-making. Certain conflicts over formal competence could be avoided by manipulating the task distribution structure, but in general it will not be possible to devise the distribution of tasks between units in such a way that each new problem falls clearly into the sphere of competence of one, and only one unit. Ways must rather be found to resolve such conflicts as they occur. Much the same is true for structurally determined conflicts over policy content. Not only can such internal conflicts not be prevented, they are important for the quality of policy, because the arguments advanced in the course of the controversy will call attention to previously neglected aspects or side-effects of a given proposal. Such conflicts should therefore not be repressed, but brought into the open, while ways and means must be found to resolve them.

If it is true that in the interest of policy itself, conflicts arising within the federal bureaucracy should be resolved rather than avoided or suppressed, this becomes a more difficult task as policy-making becomes more active. We have argued in chapter II that the level of conflict generally tends to grow with a shift from reactive to active policy-making. This holds not only for achieving external support and action consensus within the political system at large, but it also holds specifically for the federal bureaucracy. Thus, by virtue of its larger scope an active policy cuts across the existing boundaries of formal competence between sections, divisions, and even departments, and precipitates conflicts over formal competence. Conflicts over policy content will be more acute in the case of an active policy because plans to effect fundamental structural changes or a significant redistribution of values will induce the institutionalized spokesmen of the negatively affected interests to oppose them all the more strongly. For these reasons the capacity for conflict resolution in the federal bureaucracy must be higher where policy-making becomes more active, or else the processes of active policy-making will be inhibited by the very conflicts which they produce.

4.2 Anticipatory conflict resolution

We have until now talked of the intra-organizational conflicts which arise within the federal bureaucracy in the process of policy-making. But it is not only these intra-organizational conflicts which the federal bureaucracy must resolve. One of the major results of our analysis is in fact that the task of achieving action consensus and hence of resolving conflicts within the wider political action system also devolves to a large extent upon the federal bureaucracy. It is the federal departments which develop most policy proposals, and they also work to obtain an operative consensus among the relevant participants *before* the proposal is formally submitted to those who must approve of it — in sequence the cabinet, parliament, and often also the states through the *Bundesrat*.

There are several factors which constrain the bureaucracy to engage in such anticipatory conflict resolution. As for achieving consensus in the cabinet it has been pointed out previously that the principle of departmental autonomy limits decisively the powers of the cabinet as a group in making substantive policy decisions. But though the cabinet cannot take initiatives over the head of the responsible minister, it must still approve of proposals which the government has to submit to parliament. This veto function of the cabinet constrains each department to seek the agreement of other departments affected by a given proposal before submitting it to the cabinet. In general, therefore, proposals which reach the cabinet have already achieved operating consensus among the departments concerned.

Since the cabinet tends to formally submit to parliament only such proposals for legislation which are more or less certain to receive the approval of the parliamentary majority, i.e. at least of the parliamentary party groups of the majority parties, it is important for the departments to assure themselves also of the agreement of these political groups. A similar argument holds for the approval of the states where they could prevent the passage of a given piece of legislation by denying it approval in the *Bundesrat*, and it even holds for the opposition of powerful organized interests who, even though their formal approval is not needed, could still motivate ministers or political party groups to withhold their approval. Where such external opposition is clearly foreseeable or becomes visible in the early draft phases of a new program, the responsible minister will anticipate that cabinet approval may be difficult or impossible to get, and will therefore refuse to sponsor the proposal worked out in his department. This in turn motivates sections and divisions to enage in anticipatory conflict resolution with all major participants in the decision process who could themselves reject a proposal or whose opposition would motivate such rejection.

In this way considerations of external support enter into the deliberations of administrative policy-makers even though these concerns do not impinge upon them directly. These concerns are rather filtering down to them by way of the previously described process of anticipating the decision criteria of superiors who must formally adopt or reject a proposal. This extends even to considerations of popular support. Knowing that for the sake of his party and for his own political survival the minister must be sensitive to voter reactions, section heads attempt to take also this constraint into account in formulating their draft, or else division heads will impress this need upon them before passing a revised version of the original draft up to the departmental executive. The operative units will also take into consideration the effects which a given proposal, if enacted, might have on the positional interests of superiors, e.g. whether it would extend or curtail their spheres of responsibility or the means at their disposal. Considerations of general system support will be a less important constraint for administrative decisions-makers, at least as long as this resource is not becoming critically scarce and forces politicians and thus indirectly also the bureaucracy to pay attention to this particular aspect of their proposals.

In this way a complex pattern of several interlinked sets of rationality criteria develops. These criteria do not always point into the same direction, so that conflicts can arise even here. As these criteria guide the development of policy proposals within the federal departments, a process of anticipatory conflict resolution and support mobilization is initiated which establishes their focal

154

role in achieving action consensus within the political action system.

4.3 Mobilizing external support

The federal departments have two ways in which they can attempt to achieve action consensus for their projects — either by the passive anticipation of possible objections and corresponding adjustments in their propopsals, or by entering into contact with the relevant action partners and trying actively to establish consensus and mobilize support. We shall briefly consider what the federal bureaucracy does to mobilize support in the socio-economic environment.

Excluding its political top, the bureaucracy is not well suited to the task of deliberately mobilizing popular support in general, while it is very active in dealing with organized interest groups. To mobilize popular support for departmental programs, especially for programs in the preparatory stage and not yet formally decided upon, is a task which does not fit well with the traditional self-image of the civil servant. In fact, public relations work engaged in by individual civil servants below the level of divisional leadership is largely limited to an occasional paper read at a conference or an article published in a scientific journal. Top bureaucrats enjoy of course more public visibility, but the situation changes radically only where the political leadership of the bureaucracy is concerned. [26] Ministers and state secretaries speak on radio and TV to advocate or defend their departmental policies, and some ministers have developed a noticeable proficiency in public relations work to enlist popular support and advance their political fortunes.

The organizational infra-structure of systematic public relations work for departmental policies is unevenly developed. The Federal Press and Information Office is assigned the function of presenting the government and its policy to the German as well as foreign publics, and in doing so it also publicizes the achievements of individual departments. But since the aim of such publicity is to create a favorable impression of the government's record, it is not well adapted to the anticipatory mobilization of support for controversial decisions yet to be made.

Special public relations units also exist in all departments. These are generally small and sometimes only a one-man staff, though there are exceptions to this rule. The Ministry of Agriculture, for instance, has a large public relations staff which not only advertises departmental policies but also serves the agricultural lobby by advertising German agricultural products. In most cases, however, departmental public relations units are mainly concerned with the minister's own relations to the press and other mass media, arranging for interviews and preparing public statements. Occasionally a brochure is prepared which presents the ministry's past achievements and future plans. The public relations staff of most ministries lacks manpower, funds, and often the requisite specialized knowledge to make systematic use of opinion surveys and other instruments for gauging public opinion as a first step toward the development of systematic strategies for the mobilization of popular support.

Among other things this may be connected with the lack of a body of systematic knowledge about political impression management. We mentioned earlier that in attempting to anticipate voter reactions, politicians seem to proceed on rather simplified assumptions. It would be worthwhile to investigate on what assumptions about public opinion formation the public relations work of the ministries — individuals as well as specialized units — is based. It seems that while it is generally recognized that skillful political impression management can considerably influence the success or failure of a given policy initiative, it is not believed that such strategies could and ought to be taught, learned, and employed systematically. In the policy sciences, too, there have so far been hardly any serious attempts to develop a prescriptive theory of the strategies for mobilizing support and resolving conflicts in nonlaboratory, political situations.

In contrast to its relations with the public at large, the federal bureaucracy's relations with organized interest groups are well developed, firmly established, and considered an integral aspect of ministerial work. We mentioned already that The Joint Manual of Procedure suggests the consultation of organized interests in the course of preparing new legislation affecting them. Such consultation takes place in bilateral contacts or in the framework of the previously discussed mixed advisory commissions. In these commissions it is not only the bureaucracy which argues with the organized interests, but there is often also occasion for horizontal bargaining between opposed interests (e.g. producers and consumers, labor and business) involved in the same issue. In terms of achieving consensus for a determinate policy this horizontal bargaining can be quite effective. The relation between the bureaucracy and organized interests is, on the other hand, beset by a difficult problem, which results from the fact that while the consultation of organized interests aims to mobilized their support for a certain policy, obtaining such support may be predicated upon the extent to which the expressed demands of the organized interests are accepted by the policy-makers. While personal contacts and the opportunity to speak one's mind can help to mitigate a stance of opposition, experienced functionaries representing clearly defined interests will be placated only by substantive concessions. Depending on the case the consensus which is bought with a compromise may well mean to whittle down a progressive policy proposal to a small incremental program change, especially where the administrative planners attempt to serve not only the powerful vested interests but pursue a policy of redistribution and structural change in favor of underprivileged groups.

4.4 Patterns of conflict resolution

Federal bureaucrats generally agree that it is part of their job to see that policy proposals which they initiate receive the needed approval and are put into effect. Their major interaction partners in this process of seeking to establish action consensus are other units of the federal bureaucracy, interest organizations, state governments, and parliament. Where opposition is most likely to come from depends of course on the nature of a given policy initiative. There are cases where organized interests are directly affected and others where this is not true, e.g. in specific matters of criminal law reform. Where state competences are touched or a joint project must be developed, it is obviously the agreement of the states which must be obtained. The relevant set of interaction partners is therefore likely to change from issue to issue, though for a given section or division a stable pattern can develop as it deals repeatedly with problems involving similar interests.

Depending on whose agreement must be achieved, different levels of the bureaucracy become active, and these have different means of resolving conflicts at their disposal. Sections, or more particularly section heads, take care of routine contacts with interest organizations, they have contacts with state representatives if the case demands it, and they also deal at the section level with other divisions and departments. The sections' capacity for conflict resolution, i.e. their capacity to induce these interaction partners to agree to a policy initiative or at least agree not to oppose it, is quite restricted by their low-level organizational location. Section heads have no independent authority over any of their interaction partners. Their chances for bargaining successfully are slight because they do not dispose of effective sanctions and have little to offer in exchange for obtaining a compromise solution. This, at any rate, holds for policy-making where the issue is controversial and the opponent disposes of an independent base of power. In many other cases a section head and even a section assistant may be a person whom one had better not antagonize, for instance where a particular client stands in a relation of dependence to him, needing his approval or authorization on recurrent occasions. Here the bargaining position of a section would, of course, be a strong one, but the relevance of these cases for the sections' capacity to mobilize support in policy-making is limited by the fact that the potent opponents in policy issues are rarely the same persons or groups who have good reasons to respect the wishes of the section.

Sometimes a section can influence the balance of power by forming a coalition, but a section is not a very powerful and therefore not a very attractive coalition partner. Section heads must therefore mainly try to persuade their interaction partners to give up their opposition, for instance by convincing them that their fears of certain negative repercussion are unfounded. Quite in line with this, the main function of contacts among section heads is the exploration of points of opposition and the search for compatible solutions.

If the section fails and the conflict remains unresolved, the matter is often referred to the next hierarchical level and there taken up again. The Joint Manual of Procedure prescribes this for intra-departmental conflicts which cannot be resolved in horizontal contacts. This rule is applied analogously to conflicts involving an extra-departmental partner. If the conflict involves another federal department, its referrral from a section to the responsible division head in department A means that in department B it also passes up to the divisional level; the same holds for the next move up the hierarchy. Where state governments and interest organizations are concerned, there is often a similar tendency to substitute higher-ranking representatives for those who handled the matter so far as soon as it is referred up the line in the federal bureaucracy. This substitution of a completely new set of interaction partners makes it sometimes easier to come to an agreement, because the higher-ranking officials and functionaries are not strictly bound to

158

the position taken before by their subordinates and can therefore make concessions without loosing face or showing weakness.

The divisional leadership deals generally with the same type of interaction partners and the same conflicts the sections deal with, the main difference being that what is referred to the divisional level from below has become controversial already, while the contacts entered into by the sections usually start with an exploratory phase and often do not develop into conflicts. But the divisional leadership is also in a better position to resolve conflicts. Division heads can solve conflicts in their own division by authoritative decision. Toward outside partners, their bargaining chances are better than those of sections because, due to the larger volume of projects which they can influence procedurally (timing!) as well as substantively, they can negotiate more easily a favorable compromise in one matter by promising to be obliging or threatening to be intransigent in a second matter in which the same interaction partner is interested. Division heads who, instead of being career civil servants, have been externally recruited to their positions often have an additional advantage in bargaining if they have retained close relations with outside interest groups, parties, or politicians. Where division heads resort to strategies of persuasion, the new element compared to conflict resolution at the section level is the nature of their arguments, which tend to be more political, i.e. to refer to the restraints imposed by the political situation rather than to factual aspects of the issue involved. But with all this, many conflicts remain unresolved also at the divisional level and are therefore passed on to the departmental executive, in most cases to one of the state secretaries but eventually even to the minister himself.

The departmental executive and in particular the minister himself can not only solve all intra-departmental conflicts by authoritative decision, but by virtue of the elevated position disposes also of forceful sanctions which can induce recalcitrant opponents to give in once the conflict has moved up to this level. But the main point is that by virtue of being both politicians and administrators, of being fully implicated both in the federal bureaucracy and in the political system in the narrow sense (parties and parliament) and playing leading roles in both, ministers, parliamentary secretaries and politically recruited permanent secretaries are able to mobilize support in a much larger part of the whole action system than a mere administrator possibly could. A minister can activate the conflict resolution potential of the government and of parliament; he may for instance induce his party leader to exert pressure upon a colleague of the same party to agree for the sake of solidarity to a proposal he originally fought, or he may ward off the claims of an interest group by prevailing upon its (unofficial) spokesmen in parliament who are also members of his political party. In managing such coalition, departmental executives often use arguments of internal or external political support, i.e. they manage agreements by bringing new constraints to bear upon their interaction partners. This of course also works the other way around, i.e. departmental executives can similarly be compelled from the outside to renounce a claim or relinquish a project for the sake of political considerations. This mechanism was skillfully exploited during the Grand Coalition when Georg Leber, then Minister of Transportation, found his controversial program of taxing road transportation in order to subsidize the ailing railroad-system blocked in parliament by the opposition of the CDU/CSU as the larger coalition party. At this point, in the spring of 1968, the Social Democrats found themselves badly beaten in an important state election. Playing upon the intense frustration of the Social Democrats and the threatening disruption of the Grand Coalition, Leber managed to obtain CDU/CSU approval of his transportation program as a political concession that would ensure the continuation of an uneasy coalition until the end of its parliamentary term.

It does not follow necessarily, but has a certain logic that political contacts with parliament are virtually monopolized by the departmental executive. Members of the operating units will have routine contacts with parliamentary committees, where they are heard as experts, but rarely with parliamentary party groups and individual members of parliament. The importance of political relations distinguishes the executive's pattern of contacts in search of support and for the sake of conflict resolution clearly from that of the lower hierarchical levels. Section heads and to a large extent also subdivision and division heads (except for those who were externally recruited and still have personal contacts to political groups) very rarely initiate contacts to parliament, and where they do so, only with the departmental executive's prior approval. Where members of parliament contact a lower level bureaucrat on their own initiative, the latter normally informs his superior of the matter. The parliamentary contacts of the federal bureaucracy are thus much more fully controlled by its political leadership than other external relations. Moreover, most section heads and division heads are careful to limit their parliamentary contacts rather strictly to their informational purpose and will not attempt to seek political support for their projects of their own account, a task which the departmental leadership clearly reserves for itself.

The pattern of conflict resolution in the federal bureaucracy is thus characterized by two closely connected features: the concentration of the capacity for conflict resolution at the top, and the upward movement of unresolved conflicts from lower to higher levels. This upward movement holds of course especially for decentrally initiated projects or issues arising at lower organizational levels. If a centrally initiated policy meets with outside opposition in the drafting stage, the lower departmental levels have a much better stand in their negotiations because they act as emissary of the powerful departmental executive and may therefore obtain agreement more easily. Similarly, where a policy initiative forms part of the announced government program it has a better chance to find consensus, because such an announcement means that powerful participants in the action system are committed to it and can be counted on to support it.

Without such support *ex ante*, only certain kinds of conflict have a good chance of being resolved at the level of the sections and divisions. These are mainly of the intra-organizational type, involving differences of opinion resulting from divergent professional orientations, and conflicts over departmental resources and the distribution of responsibilities. In contrast, intra-organizational conflicts over policy which reflect external conflicts between socio-economic groups often prove unresolvable at the level of sections and divisions and tend therefore to converge at the top. Conflicts over policy with external participants such as organized interests, and especially the parliamentary party groups, also tend — if they are more than peripheral — to involve the departmental excutive.

The already high demands upon leadership capacity for conflict resolution is further increased by a tendency to refer not only the really difficult and "big" cases upwards, but to enlist the departmental excutive's help also for the resolution of smaller issues. In fact, the greater powers of the higher levels give them a distinct advantage in conflict resolution precisely where smaller issues are concerned. Here a direct intervention of the superior might achieve within a day what at the lower level would cost weeks of negotation or would never be fully obtained. Those who approach a department from the outside reinforce the accumulation of conflicts at the higher echelons since they often try to contact higher ranking persons instead of being content to speak to the responsible section head or even section assistant. This is particularly true for members of the minister's party, who often approach him personally even for small favors, realizing that he would be more motivated to fulfill their wishes than a nonpartisan civil servant. But it also holds for the representatives of organized interests and other groups or individuals, who are attracted by the larger power of commitment of the higher levels.

Thus reinforced, the tendency for conflicts to converge toward the top of the departmental pyramid threatens to overstrain the executive's capacity for conflict resolution dangerously. The situation is not much improved by the fact that there are also forces operating in the opposite direction of inhibiting the upward referral of unresolved issues, because these inhibitions operate by and large selectively against the development of an active policy. The lower levels realize, for instance, that they cannot expect their superiors to take over an unresolved issue as in a relay race, pursuing the lower level's intentions with more powerful means, especially if the issue is "big" and involves powerful groups. The perceived need for resolving a given conflict and the specific outcome desired often change from level to level with the dominant rationality criteria. Where a section or division may be simply concerned with getting a pet project through, the departmental executive may be much more interested not to antagonize a powerful group and may therefore make concessions which are quite contrary to the intentions of the lower level unit. The same can happen where an issue becomes part of a package deal in higher level bargaining. An issue referred upward may also be delayed so long that before the issue is resolved, the right moment for action has passed. These elements of unpredictability of what the higher levels will do motivate the lower levels to avoid the upward referral of an unresolved issue, preferring to adjust their plan to the external constraints as they perceive and experience them rather than trying to change them by enlisting the help of superiors. This means in effect that the operative units of the bureaucracy will minimize the conflict potential of their projects by adjusting their content to the opposition they meet or anticipate. More often than not, the result of such adjustments is a reactive and incremental rather than active policy.

To change this situation the capacity of the bureaucracy to mobilize such support as will be needed to obtain action consensus for a given policy would have to be increased. To a very limited extent it might also be possible to lower the incidence of certain structurally determined conflicts which arise in the process of policy-making, e.g. by changing the distribution of formal responsibilities. But provided that an active policy is desired and the basic features of the political system and the country's socio-economic structure must be taken as givens, the main strategy would have to be increasing for resolving conflicts rather than decreasing the incidence of conflicts.

It is, however, not easy to see how the bureaucracy's power of conflict resolution could be substantially increased at least at the level of sections and divisions. To be sure, new forms of coordination may enable the operative units to overcome intra- and inter-departmental conflicts more easily, and it is also conceivable that departmental public relations activities in favor of the policy developed by the operative units may be improved. But on the whole, the power of the lower bureaucratic levels vis-à-vis other participants in the policy-making process cannot be increased in correspondence with the growing incidence and intensity of conflicts as policy becomes more active, so that they must depend increasingly on the departmental executive for conflict resolution.

The question is therefore whether it would be possible to increase the departmental executive's capacity for conflict resolution by introducing organizational and procedural changes. This seems indeed feasible and a number of proposals to this effect have already been made. [27] Nor is the realization of such reform proposals without prospects, because the departmental executive disposes of the authority to secure their implementation within its own department.

But the problem of achieving action consensus and mobilizing support for active policies cannot be solved at the departmental level alone. In fact, a mere strengthening of the departmental executive without simultaneous and commensurate reinforcement of government-wide coordination and cooperation could increase inter-departmental conflicts. The crucial problem is therefore how to strengthen the capacity for conflict resolution in inter-departmental relations and in federal-state relations. In both cases hierarchical sanctions to enforce cooperation are not available. The cabinet, as we have seen, does not function as a collegial leadership. In federal-state relations, the financial sanctions of the federal government are largely ineffective as directive instruments. The conflict between the CDU/CSU majority in the *Bundesrat* and the SPD-FDP government in Bonn further impedes conflict resolution in the federal-state dimension, since in this situation all policy questions become political issues. The possibility of increasing the capacity for conflict resolution in the interest of active policies depends therefore heavily on the existing chances for structural reforms in this wider context. To these we shall turn in the final chapter.

Chapter IX

OUTLOOK: THE CHANCES FOR STRUCTURAL REFORM

1. Deficiencies

Our survey of the prerequisites of active policy-making in the federal bureaucracy has left us with a mixed impression: the defects we noted do not seem serious if measured against 'reasonable' expectations, but the demands of active policy-making are nowhere fully met.

First, the deficiencies of the classical budgetary process continue to reduce overall allocative efficiency, program effectiveness, and spending efficiency. While middle-range financial planning and the institutionalization of a second round of budget negotiations between the departments and the Ministry of Finance have helped to reduce the most glaring irrationalities of the classical process, these innovations appear to be one-shot improvements, rather than the beginning of an evolutionary transformation which would require basic changes in the relationship between central and lower-level units in the budgetary process. Central units would have to increase considerably their institutional capacity for output-oriented program analysis, review, and evaluation before they could relinquish some of their disfunctional input-oriented controls over the details of budgetary allocations. But the conditions for a strengthening of central functions in the determination of policy outputs, and of lower-level discretion in the allocation of budgetary inputs are hard to provide within the present institutional context, and changes moving in that direction are not visible.

Secondly, prevailing patterns of information gathering and information processing in the federal bureaucracy appear satisfactory only from the perspective of specialized subunits with limited capacity. Their preoccupation with narrow, well-worked areas of responsibility tends to limit the demand for scientific information regarding the dynamics of the larger socio-economic system. But if, instead of a narrow institutional perspective, one should adopt a broader functional perspective, present practices of information gathering and utilization seem grossly inadequate. Analyses of more complex and longer range societal developments and problem-generating processes are not undertaken by the specialized divisions within the departments, and if they should be produced by the science system or under commission by policy-oriented semi-independent agencies, a fragmented governmental structure would ignore the results and, at any rate, would have almost no way of generating the complex, interdependent policy patterns that more comprehensive studies would call for.

Thirdly, the prevailing practice of negative coordination reinforces the impact of a fragmented organizational structure upon information processing and problem solving processes within the bureaucracy. Positive coordination, which would join the separate perspectives and action potentials of organizational units in integrated processes of analysis and policy development, has proven extremely expensive in terms of its demands upon the capacity of communications systems. Successful positive coordination would depend upon the sophisticated management of complexity, for which neither the institutional capacity nor the procedural know-how seems available at present. Furthermore, coordination within the federal bureaucracy and, in particular, between the federal government and the states tends to discriminate against broader, more innovative policy initiatives, due to the low potentials for conflict resolution available at these levels.

In our opinion, the low capacity for conflict resolution is indeed the major constraint upon active policy-making in the Federal Republic. While proposals for increasing the effectiveness of departmental leadership may not be entirely unrealistic, significant increases in the conflict-solving potential at the government-wide and federal-state levels are nowhere in sight.

To put the matter pointedly: Our studies of policy-making in the German federal bureaucracy have persuaded us that technical, organizational, and procedural improvements of resource management, information utilization, and policy coordination are urgently needed if the capacity of the political system for active policy-making is to be increased. We are also convinced that concepts and proposals that would significantly improve the performance of the

166

policy-making system in these respects are either available and ready for introduction or could be developed within reasonable time under the pressure of sufficient demand. But this is no reason for optimism. Even if all plausible recommendations for the technical, organizational, and procedural improvement of budgeting, information processing, and coordination were realized, unresolvable policy-conflict would still prevent the achievement of truly significant increases in the level of active policy-making. Yet, reforms which would increase the capacity for conflict resolution will meet with particularly strong resistance, not because they would involve constitutional changes, but because they would go against the positional interest of major participants in the political action system. Such reforms are unlikely because they already presuppose what they are designed to produce. But without such reforms even the technical and procedural improvements in budgeting, policy analysis and coordination are hard to realize and will probably remain so. We will discuss this complex network of interlinking constraints on the chances for structural reforms in the following section.

2. Conflict resolution and structural change

We have seen that over the last few years, the federal departments have succeeded in varying degrees to introduce procedural and organizational reforms which have served to increase their information processing capacity as well as the capacity for systematic leadership involvement in policy-making processes within the department. However, departmental reforms, even if they were more extensive, are insufficient to increase the capacity for active policy-making of the political system as a whole. In fact, given the existing particularism of the departments, their increased policy-making strength may even aggravate the problem of government-wide coordination, unless complementary reforms take place at this level. But as we have seen, the more modest attempts to introduce a degree of central policy coordination through the planning division of the Chancellor's Office had to be abandoned and existing federal-state policy planning structures have increased the rigidity, rather than the flexibility, of federal-state policy coordination.

The reasons for this manifest difference in reformability between the departmental, federal, and federal-state levels seem fair-

167

ly straightforward. At the departmental level there is a special unit responsible for intra-departmental organization and reorganization, including the creation of new organizational sub-units, changes in the task allocation between existing subunits, and changes in the overall organizational structure of the ministry. True, the organization sections within division Z are often poorly staffed, their members usually lack professional training in organization and management, and they are overburdened with routine assignments such as the continuous readjustment of task allocation plans and the screening of applications for the reclassification of particular jobs. In most ministries, the organizing function is also utilized in an ad hoc fashion as an instrument of personnel policy, e.g. by creating additional sections or subdivisions in order to permit the recruitment or promotion of specific persons into higher-ranking positions. But while for these reasons the ordinary performance of organization sections may be unimpressive, a number of departments have demonstrated that it is possible to activate the organizing function and to bring about significant structural changes with important consequences for the departments' policy-making capacity. At times, the departments have managed to develop new structural patterns on their own, at other times they have called upon the assistance of the interministerial "project group for governmental and administrative reform" and of private management consulting firms. In either case, the crucial ingredient in departmental reorganization was always strong leadership involvement in the development and implementation of reorganization proposals. It seems that at the departmental level, the formal structure of hierarchical authority is still strong enough to overcome internal opposition to change if authority is employed in support of reorganization plans which are intrinsically sound and, therefore, will also find support at the rank-and-file level.

None of these favorable conditions exist at the government-wide level. Here we have, first, not one but at least five separate units claiming some authority in the area of government organization. First, there is the Chancellor's Office responsible for advising the chancellor in the exercise of his organizing power by which he defines and redefines the jurisdiction of federal ministries. Secondly, the Ministry of the Interior claims responsibility for concepts of departmental organization and for the Joint Manual of Procedure. At the same time, the Ministry of Finance in its scrutiny of budget applications for new personnel positions has developed some capacity for evaluating organizational structures; and the

168

Federal Court of Accounts reviews the efficiency of organizational arrangements in the course of its routine budget review and in its special reports on the efficiency of federal administration.

In addition, the inter-ministerial project group for governmental and administrative reform briefly mentioned above claims some authority for governmental reorganization. This project group was created in 1969 and had its life extended annually ever since. It produced the proposals upon which the reorganization attempts of the Social-Liberal coalition were based in 1970. [1] Over the years, the project group has commissioned a large number of studies of government organization and procedure, which have greatly added to the store of information available about the workings of the federal government. But its later, rather more sophisticated reports and recommendations have not found nearly the attention which its first attempt of 1969 had gained. With the exception of its work for a few individual departments, its influence on government-wide reorganization seems to have become insignificant.

But neither is there any measurable influence of the other four claimants to the organizing function at the government-wide level. Part of their ineffectiveness can surely be attributed to the competition among these units. They are all quite small and limited in their special functions, but they have always been able to prevent each one of them from expanding its area of competence and its resource base to the point where it might be able to effectively perform organizing functions for the government. At the same time, the location in separate and sometimes conflicting departments and offices has also prevented their cartellization, in spite of a common interest in the greater effectiveness of the organizing function. Within their respective departments, on the other hand, these government-wide organizing functions are invariably located at the periphery of leadership interest and attention, so that neither the Chancellor's Office, nor the Ministry of the Interior, nor the Ministry of Finance ever came forward with serious, politically credible claims to monopoly or, at least, preponderance in the field of government organization.

Such self-restraint seems altogether plausible in view of the fact that even if all of the existing fragments of the organizing function were combined into one monopoly, it would still not amount to an effective power base vis-à-vis the federal ministries. Under the present pattern of departmental particularism government-wide organizational reforms would necessarily impair departmental autonomy and would therefore be associated with relatively high levels

169

of conflict which none of the potential claimants of the organizing function could welcome. In order to be effective, government-wide policy-making structures would have to interfere with intra-departmental processes of program development — but unlike Finance, a central unit responsible for government reorganization would not dispose of effective sanctions against recalcitrant departments.

As a result, the government has received a number of highly pertinent and promising recommendations for structural change from the various bodies concerned with organizational questions. It has not, however, been able to create the institutional prerequisites which might make rationally controlled major structural changes a realistic proposition.

Still, at the governmental level the chancellor's authority and the opportunities provided by changes in the government coalition or in ministerial assignments might be utilized as an instrument for more systematic structural reforms. At the level of federal-state interactions, however, even this limited potential for unilaterally directed change is lacking. Changes in federal-state relations aiming at more effective coordination and central direction will meet with the resistance of the states safeguarding their constitutionally defined autonomy. True, the federal parliament has set up a commission of inquiry into questions of constitutional reform which is addressing itself to federal-state relations as one of its major concerns. [2] But any constitutional amendment which the commission will propose will have to be ratified by a two-thirds majority in the federal parliament as well as in the *Bundesrat*. This means that at the federal level the consent of both the government coalition and the opposition is needed, and that the consent among the states has to be nearly unanimous before structural patterns defined by the constitution could be changed. Furthermore, even structural changes through federal legislation below the constitutional level will usually require the consent of the *Bundesrat*. For all practical purposes, therefore, consent for structural changes in federal-state relations which might increase central directive capacity is extremely hard to obtain. Thus, the changes which do come about will protect, rather than encroach upon, existing veto positions and will tend to increase, rather than reduce, the level of complexity of the system and the consensus requirements of political action. This was the result of the 1969 constitutional reform, and it is the likely result of all current efforts. A decision-making structure which suffers from over-complexity and from an abundance of constraints seems intrinsically unable to reduce its degree of complexity and its internal constraints through its own decision-making procedures.

3. Chances for major reorganization

We have argued so far that specific structural conditions obstruct major organizational reforms above the departmental level which would increase the capacity of the political action system of checks and balances among groups and institutions with competitive or conflicting interests. As a consequence, there is (1) no dominant power center able to impose structural changes, while at the same time (2) voluntary self-coordination on the basis of spontaneous consensus is unlikely to occur.

Of course, the need for political consensus among divergent interests, and the difficulty of obtaining such consensus is a common characteristic of all ideologically heterogeneous, socio-economically pluralistic, and politically differentiated Western democracies. But institutional conditions in the Federal Republic increase these difficulties beyond the level that is characteristic of either the classical parliamentary systems or the American presidential system. In an ideal-type parliamentary system, ideological and socio-economic conflicts of interest are at least partly decided for a certain period by the outcome of national elections, and the winning party is able to act upon a mandate which legitimates the neglect of some interests championed by the losing party. By contrast, elections in West Germany do not usually reduce the complexity of interests to be considered. Governments tend to be coalition governments, and the function of one partner in the coalition is usually defined as looking after those interests which the other partner is inclined to neglect. Moreover, West Germany's peculiar type of federalism adds to the range of interests that must be taken into account in federal policy-making by constraining the federal government to obtain the consensus of state governments controlled by the opposition party. Furthermore, the federal government itself consists of a plurality of semi-independent actors. The chancellorship does not provide the unifying potential of the American Presidency; ministers are political power centers with their own parliamentary base, rather than 'secretaries' assisting the President in the execution of his program. As a consequence, heterogeneous political interests are so closely associated with institutional veto positions that they cannot be reduced by either the outcome of general elections or by the political fiat of the chief of government. Under such conditions, political conflicts of interest result more easily in decision-making deadlocks than in other pluralistic democracies.

The situation is aggravated by the fact that political support for major structural reforms is even more difficult to obtain than for most substantive policy decisions, because structural reforms may permanently change the power balance between the participants in the action system. Thus, the need to increase the system's capacity for active policy-making is felt less acutely by each participant in the political action system than the threat posed to his positional interests by structural reforms. In theory, everyone would of course agree that the ability of the political system to prevent crises before they arisese, and to introduce large-scale innovations and social reforms is crucially important. But the costs which at least some political groups would incur by agreeing to major structural reforms would outweigh their political benefits which might be long-run rather than short-run, and which would probably accrue to the whole population. On the other hand, the threat of system crises and of the inability to deal effectively with a growing problem load is vague, uncertain, and far away if measured in terms of the remaining political live of present power holders. The situation seems to resemble patterns analyzed by Mancur Olsen, or by game-theoretic studies of the "prisoners' dilemma", were collectively rational decisions are counteracted by individually unfavorable cost-benefit ratios. [3]

It may thus appear that only the urgency of imminent crisis could provide the impulse for major structural reforms. However, it would be particularly difficult to introduce structural reforms in times of acute crisis, because to change a system already operating under stress might cause its sudden collapse. Besides, every manifest crisis calls first of all for its own direct solution, and under the pressure of overcoming the acute economic, educational, or environmental crisis their remote cause, the political system's deficient directive capacity, may easily be lost from sight. Furthermore, the differential impact of crisis conditions upon different parts of the electorate will tend to disintegrate rather than unify the government coalition itself. Thus, even consensus on substantive policy is unlikely to increase very much under crisis conditions.

Thus, in the Federal Republic, action consensus is likely to occur mainly as the result of the slow diffusion of a sense of urgency of a problem, and a sense of direction for promising problem solutions among the political elites in a great many separate and competing institutions. Active policies, including those of government reforms, are likely to be adopted only if politicians and bureaucrats within the government coalition, the opposition parties, and state governments have come to define a given problem more or less in the same terms and to seek its solution in the same direction. In a sense, problem solutions will not occur before they have become trivial. Of course, they may be facilitated by the ideological mobilization of public opinion for particular problems and demands; indeed the mobilization of the wider political community may be an essential precondition for the concertation of élite perceptions in the face of positional conflicts of interest. But a strategy of mobilization also entails the risk of raising expectations to an unrealistically high level which would only produce frustration and discontent. In fact, something like this has already happened in the Federal Republic, where the first large-scale reforms in the areas of financial planning, government-wide coordination, and federal-state coordination were undertaken with great optimism. Obviously, however, these innovations had not been sufficiently thought through with respect to their unlikely success and remote effects. As a consequence, unwarranted reform optimism was met with inevitable disappointment when the reforms failed to achieve the experted results. The result has been a sense of resignation and disbelief in the efficacy of structural reforms to bring about noticeable improvements.

Thus, the Federal Republic's most likely chance for self-transformation to increase active policy-making capacity remains the slow, unspectacular diffusion of political ideas among decision makers of different ideological orientations and with different positional interests at various bureaucratic and political levels. When the need for active problem solving has become the orthodoxy of even the more conservative participants in the policy-making process, structural reforms which at present seem inachievable eventually find the necessary support. Whether this conclusion bodes ill depends on developments which cannot be safely predicted. As long as a largely reactive style of policy-making which does not overstrain available financial, informational, and political resources suffices to keep the system going at present levels of performance, or as long as problems grow slowly enough to permit ad hoc mobilization of action consensus, the failure of

173

structural reforms to increase problem-solving capacity may not be dangerous. But should our expectation of rapidly increasing problem loads within the near future turn out to be true, the Federal Republic's political system seems ill prepared to deal effectively with it.

NOTES

Chapter I

1) D.H. Meadows, D.L. Meadows, J. Randers, W.W. Behrens III: The Limits to Growth. New York, Universe Books, 1972; E. Goldsmith et al.: A Blueprint fur Survival. London, Stacy, 1972.
2) F.E. Emery, E.L. Trist: The Causal Texture of Organizational Environments. Human Relations, 18, (1965), p. 21 ff.
3) W. Ross Ashby: An Introduction to Cybernetics. London, Chapman & Hall, 1956, 4th ed., pp. 206 ff.
4) Fritz W. Scharpf: Demokratietheorie zwischen Utopie und Anpassung. Konstanz, Universitätsverlag, 1970; A.S. McFarland: Power and Leadership in Pluralist Systems. Stanford, Stanford U.P., 1969.
5) Renate Mayntz, Fritz W. Scharpf: Kriterien, Voraussetzungen und Einschränkungen aktiver Politik, in: Mayntz/Scharpf (eds.), Planungsorganisation. Die Diskussion um die Reform von Regierung und Verwaltung des Bundes. München, Piper, 1973.
6) For a general description of the West-German political and social system, see, e.g.: Thomas Ellwein: Das Regierungssystem der Bundesrepublik Deutschland. Köln, Westdeutscher Verlag, 3rd ed., 1973; Lewis J. Edinger: Politics in Germany: Attitudes and Processes. Boston, Little, Brown, 1968; Gerhard Loewenberg: Parliament in the German Political System. Ithaca, N.Y., Cornell U.P., 1967; Ralph Dahrendorf: Society and Democracy in Germany. Garden City, N.Y., Doubleday, 1967; Graham Hallett: The Social Economy of West-Germany. London, Macmillan, 1973. The most recent relevant publication is Nevil Johnson: Government in the Federal Republic of Germany — The Executive at Work. Oxford et al., Pergamon Press, 1973, which became available when this book went into print.

Chapter II

1) Dieter Schröder: Die Grössenordnung der öffentlichen Ausgaben für die Infrastruktur in der Bundesrepublik Deutschland bis 1985, in: Reimut Jochimsen/Udo E. Simonis (eds.), Theorie und Praxis der Infrastrukturpolitik. Berlin, Duncker & Humblot, 1970, pp. 427 ff.

2) Andrew Shonfield: Modern Captitalism. London, Weidenfeld & Nicholson, 1965.

3) Bund-Länder-Kommission für Bildungsplanung (ed.): Bildungsgesamtplan, Vol. 1, Stuttgart, Klett, 1973, pp. 96 ff. See also the following official reports: Gesundheitsbericht der Bundesregierung, Bundestags-Drucksache VI/1667 vom 18. Dezember, 1970; Sozialbericht 1971 der Bundesregierung, Bundestags-Drucksache VI/2155 vom 15. Mai 1970; Bildungsbericht 1970 der Bundesregierung, Bundestags-Drucksache VI/925 vom 12. Juni 1970; Raumordnungsbericht 1970 der Bundesregierung, Bundestags-Drucksache VI/1340 vom 4. November 1970; Verkehrsbericht 1970 der Bundesregierung, Bundestags-Drucksache VI/1350 vom 4. November 1970; Umweltprogramm der Bundesregierung Bundestags-Drucksache VI/2710 vom 14. Oktober 1971.

4) Langzeitprogramm der SPD, Vol. 1, Texte: Entwurf eines ökonomisch-politischen Orientierungsrahmens für die Jahre 1973-1985. Bonn, Verlag Neue Gesellschaft, 1972, T2 265.

5) See generally, Albrecht Zunker: Finanzplanung und Bundeshaushalt. Zur Koordinierung und Kontrolle durch den Bundesfinanzminister. Frankfurt/Main, Metzner, 1972.

6) See for instance M. Alexis, Ch. Wilson: Information Processing for Decision Making, in: iid. (eds.): Organizational Decision Making. Englewood Cliffs, N.J., Prentice Hall Inc., 1967, pp. 312-337; J.C. Emery: Organizational Planning and Control Systems — Theory and Technology. London, Macmillan, 1969, chapts. 3 and 4.

7) This obviously includes knowledge about human behavior; the term "system dynamics" does not imply the possibility of gaining knowledge of highly aggregated system variables without reference to individual behavior and its determinants.

8) Aside from this a system of imperative control could in fact not act upon the assumption of full compliance in designing the system for planned outcomes, since it tends to provoke the wide-spread use of evasive tactics (instead of outright disobedience which the enforcement apparatus could deal with). Evasive behavior, paying merely lip-service to a norm or fulfilling it to the letter and not its intention etc., acts like sand in the system. Successful control would therefore require the additional ability to predict the extent and direction of evasive behavior and take this into account.

9) Viz. Jay W. Forrester: Urban Dynamics. Cambridge Mass., M.I.T. Press, 1969; a German application of this approach is BESI — Berliner Simulationsmodell, 1. und 2. Zwischenbericht, ZBZ-Bericht 4, 6, both 1969; Entwurf eines kommunalen Management-Systems — Berliner Simulationsmodell BESI, ZBZ-Bericht 9, 1970; all published in mimeographed form by Zentrum Berlin für Zukunftforschung, Berlin. The bestknown example of this approach on a macro-scale is of course D.H. Meadows, D.L. Meadows, J. Randers, W.W. Behrens III: The Limits to Growth. New York, Universe Books, 1972.

10) In 1972, 2.4% of the Federal Republic's GNP were spent on research and development; public funds pay for about half of these espenditures. See Forschungsbericht IV der Bundesregierung. Bonn, Bundesminister für Bildung und Wissenschaft, 1972, table 25, and the figures given by Horst

Ehmke in Bulletin No. 150 of November 23, 1973, pp. 1492-96. Bonn, Presse- und Informationsamt der Bundesregierung.

11) See for this the study of Joachim Hirsch: Wissenschaftlichtechnischer Fortschritt und politisches System. Frankfurt/Main, Suhrkamp Verlag, 1970.

12) Thus the Deutsche Forschungsgemeinschaft spent only 12% of the funds allocated in 1972 to the so-called Sonderforschungsbereiche for the humanities, social sciences, and economics altogether; viz. DFG-Mitteilungen No. 2/1972. Over 80% of the total DFG-budget go into natural and engineering sciences, medicine and agrarian science; see Hirsch, op. cit. p. 157. The Max-Planck-Gesellschaft concentrates at least as strongly on natural science research, while the federal government spends only a small fraction of its research funds for social science research, focussing strongly on certain special areas of natural science and technology; see Hirsch, op. cit., and Forschungsbericht IV der Bundesregierung, op. cit.

13) See Jürgen Raschert: Uber die Realisierbarkeit bildungspolitischer Entscheidungen. Dissertation 1973, to be published.

14) Heinz Laufer: Verfassungsgerichtsbarkeit und politischer Prozess. Studien zum Bundesverfassungsgericht der BRD. Tübingen, Mohr, 1968; Axel Görlitz: Verwaltungsgerichtsbarkeit in Deutschland. Neuwied, Luchterhand, 1970; Fritz W. Scharpf: Die politischen Kosten des Rechtsstaates. Tübingen, Mohr, 1970, pp. 38 ff.

15) This position was developed by Walter Eucken: Grundsätze der Wirtschaftspolitik. Hamburg, Rowohlt, 1959, 2nd. ed.; Alfred Müller-Armack: Soziale Marktwirtschaft, in: Handwörterbuch der Sozialwissenschaft, Vol. 9, Stuttgart, Tübingen, Göttingen, Fischer/Mohr/Vandenhoeck, 1965, and was popularized by the first Minister of Economic Affairs, see Ludwig Erhard: Wohlstand für alle. Düsseldorf, Econ, 1957.

16) E.E. Schattschneider: The Semisovereign People. A Realist's View of Democracy in America. New York, Holt, Rinehart and Winston, 1960, p. 33; Peter Bachrach/Morton Baratz: Decisions and Nondecisions: An Analytical Framework, American Political Science Review, 57 (1963), pp. 632 ff.

17) Statistisches Bundesamt (ed.), Statistisches Jahrbuch für die Bundesrepublik Deutschland, Stuttgart, Kohlhammer, 1970, p. 496.

18) See, Karlheinz Neunreither: Politics and Bureaucracy in the West German Bundesrat, American Political Science Review, 53 (1959), pp. 713 ff.; Heinz Laufer: Der Bundesrat. Untersuchungen über Zusammensetzung, Arbeitsweise, politische Rolle und Reformprobleme. Bonn, Schriftenreihe der Bundeszentrale für politische Bildung, 1972.

19) Karl-Heinrich Hansmeyer: Die Finanzverfassung der Gemeinden. Ein Beitrag zur Stellung der Gemeinden in der Finanzverfassung des Bundes. Stuttgart, Kohlhammer, 1969.

20) Günter Kisker: Kooperation im Bundesstaat. Tübingen, Mohr, 1971.

21) Enquete-Kommission des Deutschen Bundestages für Fragen der Verfassungsreform. Zwischenbericht vom 21. September 1972, Bundestags-Drucksache VI/3829.

22) Neugliederungs-Kommission 1973. Bundesminister des Innern (ed.): Bericht der Sachverständigenkommission für die Neugliederung des Bundesgebietes. Göttingen, Schwartz, 1973.

177

23) See for instance Gabriel A. Almond and G.B. Powell: Comparative Politics — A Developmental Approach. Boston, 1966, especially p. 199. More recently Warren F. Ilchman and Norman T. Uphoff have underscored the focal importance of support as a political resource in their book The Political Economy of Change. Berkeley, Univ. of Calif. Press, 1971; see esp. p. 92 where they call support the most generalized political currency.

24) Such independent variation of general system support and the support of specific policies, expressed in the balance of satisfaction/dissatisfaction with the actual policy output, is also recognized in the work of Gabriel A. Almond and Sidney Verba: The Civic Culture. Princeton, N.J., University Press, 1963.

25) Almond and Verba, op. cit.

26) 8% in Hessen 1966, 9% in Bremen 1967, 10% in Baden-Württemberg 1968. See Heino Kaack: Geschichte und Struktur des deutschen Parteiensystems. Köln, Westdeutscher Verlag, 1971, p. 302 ff.

27) Max Kaase; Analyse der Wechselwähler in der Bundesrepublik, in: Erwin K. Scheuch/Rudolf Wildenmann (eds.): Zur Soziologie der Wahl. Köln, Westdeutscher Verlag, 2nd. ed. 1968, pp. 113 ff.; sets the proportion in the 1961 federal elections at 10-15 percent of the electorate; For 1969 Hans D. Klingemann/Franz Urban Pappi; Die Wählerbewegungen bei den Bundestagswahlen am 28. September 1969. Politische Vierteljahresschrift, 11 (1970), pp. 11 ff, at 11 percent; For 1972 Jürgen W. Falter: Die Bundetagswahl vom 19. November 1972. Zeitschrift für Parlamentsfragen, 4 (1973), pp. 115 ff., at 15 percent. In contradiction to American analyses German studies emphasize that voters changing their party allegiance from one election to the next are characterized by a relatively high social status and by a political engagement above average.

28) See Heino Kaack: Fraktionswechsel und Mehrheitsverhältnisse im Deutschen Bundestag, in: Zeitschrift für Parlamentsfragen, 3 (1972), p. 138 f. The next three defections which reduced the majority of the government coalition to zero took place within the following 20 months.

29) See Bruno S. Frey: Umweltökonomie. Gottingen, Vandenhoek & Rupprecht, 1972.

30) This even holds for the meta-policy approach of Y. Dror, viz. his book Public Policy-Making Reexamined. San Francisco, Chandler, 1968.

Chapter III

1) Heino Kaack: Geschichte und Structuren des deutschen Parteiensystems. Köln, Westdeutscher Verlag, 1972.

2) Arnold J. Heidenheimer: Adenauer and the CDU. Den Haag, M. Nijhoff, 1960.

3) Wolf Dieter Narr: CDU-SPD. Program and Praxis seit 1945. Stuttgart, Kohlhammer, 1967.

4) Harold K. Schellenger: The SPD in the Bonn Republic. A Socialist Party Modernizes. Den Haag, M. Nijhoff, 1968.

5) Jürgen Domes: Bundesregierung und Mehrheitsfraktion. Köln, Westdeutscher Verlag, 1964.

6) Winfried Steffani: Amerikanischer Kongress und deutscher Bundestag — ein Vergleich, in: Kurt Kluxen (ed.), Parlamentarismus. Köln, Berlin, Kiepenheuer & Witsch, 1967, pp. 230 ff.

7) Edward Pinney: Federalism, Bureaucracy, and Party Politics in Western Germany. The Role of the Bundesrat. Chapel Hill, North Carolina U.P., 1963.

8) Heinz Laufer: Der Bundesrat als Institution der Opposition. Zeitschrift für Parlamentsfragen, 1 (1970), pp. 318 ff.; Peter Schindler: Der Bundesrat in parteipolitischer Auseinandersetzung. Zeitschrift für Parlamentsfragen, 3 (1972), pp. 148 ff.

9) See the figures of legislative initiatives. Thomas Ellwein/Axel Görlitz: Parlament und Verwaltung. Vol. 1. Gesetzgebung und politische Kontrolle. Stuttgart, Kohlhammer, 1967, p. 83.

10) Ernst Wolfgang Böckenförde: Die Organisationsgewalt im Bereich der Regierung. Berlin, Duncker & Humblot, 1964.

11) Sigfried Schöne: Von der Reichskanzlei zum Bundeskanzleramt. Berlin, Duncker & Humblot, 1968; Günther Behrendt: Das Bundeskanzleramt. Frankfurt/Main, Athenäum, 1967.

12) Harm Prior: Die interministeriellen Ausschüsse der Bundesministerien. Eine Untersuchung zum Problem der Koordinierung heutiger Regierungsarbeit. Stuttgart, G. Fischer, 1968.

Chapter IV

1) This amounts to 12% of the gainfully employed in the Federal Republic. See Studienkommission für die Reform des öffentlichen Dienstrechts, Bericht der Kommission. Baden-Baden, Nomos Verlag, 1973, p. 52 ff. Before concluding prematurely that with such a large public sector the Federal Republic must be thoroughly bureaucratized, one should take into account that more than one quarter of these 3.2 mill. belong to the Federal Postal Service and the Federal Railroad.

2) See Studienkommission für die Reform des öffentlichen Dienstrechts, op. cit.; it is not likely, though, that this recommendation will soon be realized since there is a fierce controversy about the model upon which a uniform public service should be based.

3) Thomas Ellwein, Ralf Zoll: Berufsbeamtentum — Anspruch und Wirklichkeit. Düsseldorf, Bertelsmann Universitätsverlag, 1973, pp. 160-175.

4) Niklas Luhmann, Renate Mayntz: Personal im öffentlichen Dienst — Eintritt und Karrieren. Baden-Baden, Nomos Verlag, 1973, chapter 11. This research was commissioned by the Civil Service Reform Commission.

5) For these and other data used here see the statistical information given by the Studienkommission für die Reform des öffentlichen Dienstrechts, op. cit., pp. 52-87.

6) See: Arbeitsplatzstruktur und Laufbahnreform im öffentlichen Dienst. Institut für sozialwissenschaftliche Forschung, München. Research Report prepared for the Civil Service Reform Commission. Baden-Baden, Nomos Verlag, 1973.

7) See Wilhelm Bleek: Von der Kameralausbildung zum Juristenprivileg. Berlin, Colloquium Verlag, 1972.

8) See Gerhard Brinkmann: Die Diskriminierung der Nicht-Juristen im allgemeinen höheren Verwaltungsdienst der BRD. Zeitschrift für die gesamte Staatswissenschaft, 129 (1973), pp. 150-167, who shows that the average income (and hence the average rank) of jurists is significantly higher than of all other comparable groups with an academic training, age being kept constant. This result is supported by the study of Luhmann and Mayntz who found that jurists are clearly over-represented among higher civil servants who have reached top positions; op. cit., p. 142.

9) See for this part I of the study by Luhman and Mayntz, op. cit.

10) See N. Luhmann, R. Mayntz, op. cit., p. 255 f.

11) N. Luhmann, R. Mayntz, op. cit., pp. 140-150; the characteristics measured included such personality dimensions as dogmatism, intolerance of ambiguity, dominance, reactive speed, etc., but also performance in earlier examinations and some career variables.

12) In the terminology used by D. Katz and R.L. Kahn: The Social Psychology of Organizations. New York, Wiley, 1966, chapter 12.

13) See Luhmann and Mayntz, op. cit., chapter 9.

14) Luhmann and Mayntz, op. cit., p. 240.

15) See for instance J. Fiedler: The Doctrine of Political Neutrality of the German Higher Civil Service — A Reassessment. Berkeley, University Press, 1969; and John Herz: Political Views of the West German Civil Service, in: Hans Speier and W. Phillip Davison (eds.): West German Leadership and Foreign Policy. New York, Row, Peterson & Co., 1957.

16) Robert D. Putnam: The Political Attitudes of Senior Civil Servants in Western Europe — A preliminary Report. British Journal of Political Science, 3 (1973), pp. 257-290.

17) Putnam, op. cit., p. 260.

18) See for the following Luhmann and Mayntz, op. cit., chapter 11.

19) The same phenomenon of a pronounced attitudinal difference between generations has once more been shown also in the study by Ellwein and Zoll, op. cit., p. 182.

20) Peter Grottian: Zum Planungsbewusstsein der Bonner Ministerialbürokratie — Vorläufige Ergebnisse einer empirischen Studie. Politische Vierteljahresschrift, Sonderheft No. 4, Vol. 13, 1972.

Chapter V

1) Niklas Luhmann/Renate Mayntz: Personal im öffentlichen Dienst — Eintritt und Karrieren. Baden-Baden, Nomos Verlagsgesellschaft, 1973.

2) See Manfred Lepper: Die Basiseinheit in der Organisation der Ministerien, in: Organisation der Ministerien des Bundes und der Länder, Schriftenreihe der Hochschule Speyer, Band 52. Berlin, Dunker and Humblot, 1973, p. 132. Lepper points out that the average size of the sections in the federal ministeries is even relatively large compared to that of sections in the state ministeries.

3) Ira Sharkansky: Public Administration. Chicago, Markham Publ. Co., 2nd ed., 1972, p. 59.

4) See Manfred Lepper: Teams in der öffentlichen Verwaltung, in: Die Verwaltung, 5 (1972), pp. 141-172.

5) At the national level ("Reich") this institution dates back to 1899; it meant in fact merely a — limited — revival of what used to be the normal status of civil servants in the period of absolutist rule.

6) See Josef Kölble: Die Organisation der Führungszwischenschicht in den Ministerien, in: Aktuelle Probleme der Ministerialorganisation, Vol. 48 of the Schriftenreihe der Hochschule für Verwaltungswissenschaften Speyer. Berlin, Duncker & Humblot, 1972, p. 182 f.

7) Joseph L. Bower: Managing The Resource Allocation Process — A Study of Corporate Planning and Investment. Boston, Graduate School of Business Administration, Harvard University, 1970.

8) Heinz Laufer: Der parlamentarische Staatssekretär — Eine Studie über ein neues Amt der Bundesregierung. München, Beck Verlag, 1969.

Chapter VII

1) The system of planning commissioners is briefly described by Klaus Seemann: Das Verhältnis von Aufgabenplanung und Finanzplanung in einer Planungskonzeption für Regierung und Verwaltung. Verein für Verwaltungsreform und Verwaltungsforschung, Bonn (undated), pp. 12-13; see also Horst Ehmke: Computer helfen der Politik. Die Zeit, December 17, 1971, p. 7.

2) See: Projektgruppe Regierungs- und Verwaltungsreform: Dritter Bericht zur Reform der Struktur von Bundesregierung und Bundesverwaltung. Bonn, 1972, I/18 ff.

3) The developments briefly described in this section are discussed in great detail by Heribert Schatz: Auf der Suche nach neuen Problemlösungsstrategien — Die Entwicklung der politischen Planung auf Bundesebene, in: R. Mayntz, F.W. Scharpf (eds.): Planungsorganisation — Die Diskussion um die Reform von Regierung und Verwaltung des Bundes. München, Piper Verlag, 1973. For his analysis Schatz has drawn on published and unpublished material as well as on knowledge personally gained as former member of the Chancellor's Office; see there for further bibliographic references.

4) For a more detailed analysis of this system of financial planning see Schatz, op. cit.; Seemann op. cit.; K.-H. Hansmeyer, Bert Rürup: Staatwirtschaftliche Planungsinstrumente. Tübingen, J.C.B. Mohr (Paul Siebeck) Verlag, Düsseldorf, Werner Verlag, 1973; Frieder Naschold: Probleme der mehrjährigen Finanzplanung des Bundes, in: V. Ronge, G. Schmieg (eds.): Politische Planung in Theorie und Praxis. München, Piper Verlag, 1971.

5) In addition to Schatz, op. cit., see for this reform also Alfred Faude: Regierungs- und Verwaltungsreform beim Bund; Reimut Jochimsen: Zum Aufbau und Ausbau eines integrierten Aufgabenplanungs- und Koordinationssystems der Bundesregierung, both in: J.H. Kaiser (ed.):

Planung VI. Baden-Baden, Nomos Verlag, 1972; see also Horst Ehmke: Planung im Regierungsbereich, in: F. Naschold, W. Väth (eds.): Politische Planungssysteme. Köln, Westdeutscher Verlag, 1973.

Chapter VIII

1) James O'Connor: The Fiscal Crisis of the State. Socialist Revolution, Vol. 1, 1970.
2) Aaron Wildavsky: The Politics of the Budgetary Process. Boston, Little, Brown, 1964; Joachim Hirsch: Haushaltplanung und Haushaltskontrolle. Stuttgart, Kohlhammer 1968.
3) Albrecht Zunker: Finanzplanung und Bundeshaushalt. Frankfurt a.M., Metzner Verlag, 1972.
4) Aaron Wildavsky: Budgeting. Forthcoming.
5) See: PROGNOS AG: Die öffentliche Förderung kleiner und mittlerer Unternehmen. Studie im Auftrag des Bundesministerium der Finanzen, Basel 1971; Deutsches Institut für Wirtschaftsforschung, PROGNOS A.G., et al.: Enquete über die Bauwirtschaft. Im Auftrag des Bundesministeriums für Wirtschaft, Berlin, 1973; PROGNOS A.G.: Förderungsmassnahmen zur Verbesserung der Molkereistruktur. Kosten-Nutzen-Analyse. Im Auftrag des Bundesministeriums für Landwirtschaft, Basel, 1974.
6) William A. Niskanen: Bureaucracy and Representative Government. Chicago, Aldine, Atherton 1971, p. 133.
7) Responsibility for science policy is divided since 1973 between the Ministry of Education and Science, mainly responsible for university research, and the new Ministry of Research and Technology. Of course the large research budgets of other departments also have a considerable effect upon the government's overall science policy.
8) Eberhard Witte: Das Informationsverhalten in Entscheidungsprozessen. Tübingen, J.C.B. Mohr, 1972. The study is based on the analysis of 233 comparable decisions made mainly by industrial managers and on some laboratory experiments with management games, where Witte showed that only between 6% and 11% (at the third trial) of the information held available and needed for an optimal solution were actually requested by participants.
9) This is true even though the states are obliged by the constitution to give information to the federal government.
10) See the announcement in the Social Report for 1971, Bundestagdrucksache VI/2155, p. 46. As a first result of ongoing work a volume "Gesellschaftliche Daten 1973 in der Bundesrepublik Deutschland" has been published in October 1973 by the Federal Press Office.
11) Hannes Friedrich: Staatliche Verwaltung und Wissenschaft- Die wissenschaftliche Beratung der Politik aus der Sicht der Ministerialbürokratie. Frankfurt/Main, Europäische Verlagsanstalt, 1970, p. 48.
12) There exists also a third, highly specialized type of commission (Fachbeiräte), which is found more frequently than scientific commissions; in addition to providing specialized information this type of commission

often fulfills delegated administrative tasks, for instance setting up certain technical norms. From the point of view of the informational requirements of an active policy this type of commission is of little interest here.

13) GGO II, op. cit., §23.

14) The Joint Manual makes such selectivity a rule; viz. GGO I, op. cit., §77.

15) See Fritz W. Scharpf: Fallstudien zu Entscheidungsprozessen in der Bundesregierung, in: R. Mayntz, F.W. Scharpf (eds.): Planungsorganisation. München, Piper, 1973. Similar results were reported by R.A. Bauer, J. de Sola Pool, L.A. Dexter: American Business and Public Policy — The Politics of Foreign Trade. New York, Atherton Press, 1963.

16) Joachim Hirsch: Wissenschaftlich-technischer Fortschritt und politisches System. Frankfurt, Suhrkamp Verlag, 1970, p. 129 f; the states maintain another 86 research institutions and experimental stations.

17) Friedrich, op. cit., p. 224 ff. This is an interview study concluded in 1966, involving 103 intensive interviews with senior civil servants from 14 federal ministeries who on their official capacity have to deal with various forms of getting scientific information and advice.

18) Friedrich, op. cit., p. 130 ff.

19) Friedrich, p. 162 ff.

20) See Alfred Faude: Datenverarbeitung und Verwaltungspersonal. Report delivered at the International Institute of Administrative Sciences' colloquium at Nice in 1973; the figures for the personnel refer to 1972.

21) See Winfried Roth: Informatik und staatliches Kassen- und Rechnungswesen. Report delivered at the International Institute of Administrative Sciences' colloquium at Nice in 1973. For the following see also the report delivered at the same occasion by Klaus Lenk: Information und Verwaltungsentscheidung; and Joachim Hirsch: Wissenschaftlich-technischer Fortschritt und politisches System. Frankfurt/Main, Suhrkamp Verlag, 1970, pp. 179-183.

22) See the study by Harm Prior: Die interministeriellen Ausschüsse der Bundesministerien. Eine Untersuchung zum Problem der Koordinierung heutiger Regierungsarbeit. Stuttgart, G. Fischer, 1968.

23) Fritz W. Scharpf: Komplexität als Schranke der politischen Planung. Politische Vierteljahresschrift, 13 (1972), Sonderheft 4, p. 168 ff.

24) Institute for Operational Research/Fritz W. Scharpf et. al.: Methoden der Problemstrukturierung. Positive Koordination in der Langfristplanung. Untersuchungsbericht erstellt für die Projektgruppe Regierungs- und Verwaltungsreform. Bonn, 1972, mimeo.

25) Fritz W. Scharpf: Alternativen des deutschen Föderalismus. Die Neue Gesellschaft, 1974, Heft 3.

26) Some strategies which the bureaucracy might use in this context are discussed by Leon V. Sigal: Bureaucratic Objectives and Tactical Uses of the Press. Public Administration Review, 33 (1973), pp. 336-345.

27) See the specific proposals made by the authors in the chapter entitled "Vorschläge zur Reform der Ministerial-organisation", in: Renate Mayntz, Fritz W. Scharpf (eds.); Planungsorganisation, München, Piper Verlag, 1973.

Chapter IX

1) Projektgruppe Regierungs- und Verwaltungsreform beim Bundesminister des Innern: Erster Bericht zur Reform der Struktur von Bundesregierung und Bundesverwaltung. Bonn, August 1969 (mimeographed).
2) Zwischenbericht der Enquête-Kommission zu Fragen der Verfassungsreform. Bundestags-Drucksache VI/3829, Bonn, 1972.
3) Mancur Olson: The Logic of Collective Action. Cambridge, Mass., Harvard U.P., 1965; Anatol Rapoport: Prisoner's Dilemma. A study in Conflict and Cooperation. Ann Arbor, University of Michigan Press, 1965; Thomas C. Schelling: The Strategy of Conflict. Cambridge, Mass., Harvard U.P., 1963.